CONTENTS

Hello wonderful readers

Welcome to the last issue of Amelia's Magazine, at least as it currently exists. It's been an amazing five years, but I always planned to do ten issues then see how I felt, and the time has come to move on... I have loads of new ideas that I just don't have time to work on right now, plus I need to find other jobs to pay off all my debts. The magazine will stay online, and continue to grow as a must-stop-and-see resource for all things inspiring: Creativity in the Climate of Change. I hope you'll sign up to my mailing list for weekly updates.

For this final print issue I've pulled out all the stops: you can read about my trip to India at the back of the magazine, there's an online compilation of exclusive music from featured artists hosted on Last.fm, and of course you get a fabulous FREE* fairtrade bag kit. Get that sewing machine out now!

lots of love

♥ AmelBax

*whilst stocks last

Publisher, Editor and Art Director
Amelia Gregory www.ameliagregory.com

Music Editor **Charles Drakeford**
Fashion Editor **Melinda Neunie**
Art Editor **Tanya Geddes**
Sub Editor **Ursula Raeburn**
Cover illustration **Msxi**
Bag kit **Brie Harrison**
Design and Editorial **Dearbhaile Kitt, Emma Hamshare, Kate Webster, Michelle Heimerman, Sarah Barnes**
Design **Abigail Aked, Chery Hang Nguyen, Val Sarakitprija**

Get in touch
art@ameliasmagazine.com
earth@ameliasmagazine.com
fashion@ameliasmagazine.com
music@ameliasmagazine.com

Special thanks
To Carhartt and Paul Smith, who have faithfully advertised with me for so many years, and to my parents mummy and Bruce for accepting that I may never have a proper job
Thanks to Sponsors
Martin, Alan, Mark and Ken at my printers Principal Colour, who have been so brilliantly supportive of my madcap ideas since the very beginning, Justin at Fenner for providing me with such great paper, Sam and Richard for the website, Rupert and Fiona at Last.fm, Brie and Abi for making the bag happen

Contributors
Adrian Fleet, Alex Cunningham, Amy Gwatkin, Annie Collinge, Antonia Leslie, Aya Sekine, Beth Richards, Bohdan Cap, Brendan Peer, Britta Burger, Cat Lauigan, Catherine McColl, Chiara Romagnoli, David Chivall, David Fairweather, David Poole, Emma Macfarlane, Frankie Kane, Gemma Booth, Gerald Jenkins, Harris Elliott, Hayereyah, Helen Dodsworth, Jacob Denno, Jacqueline Wagner, Jane Mcleish-Kelsey, Jenny Lewis, Jess Wilson, Jessica Dance, Joan Campbell, Julia Kennedy, Julieta Sans, Kai Chan, Kate Slater, Katie Burnett, Katie Green, Kayoko Ishikawa, Laura Quick, Lauren Towner, Laurie Storey, Lilia Toncheva-O'Rourke, Lucy Barrett, Lucy Fine, Matt Bramford, Msxi, Nadine Sanders, Nat Miller, Natalia Skobeeva, Nikki Pinder, Oxana Korsun, Patrick Glen, Patrick Johansson, Paul Hanford, Paul Paper, Retts Wood, Richard Pearmain, Robin Jonsson, Ruth Holland, Sarah May, Sofia Andersson, Sophie Hill, Susie Lloyd, Tarryn Paul, Tom Howard, Will Sanders, Yelena Bryksenkova, Yoko Furusho, Yuki Kishino, Zeroten

Read the online magazine and buy back issues and artwork at:
www.ameliasmagazine.com

www.myspace.com/ameliasmagazine
Facebook group: **Amelia's Magazine**
Last.fm: **AmeliasMagazine**

EXCLUSIVE ORIGINAL LIV
CONCERT VIDEOS AND INTERVIEW!

PORTISHEAD-
MC5-
BLACK DEVIL DISCO CLUB- FAUST-
METRONOMY- DAS POP-
LIGHTSPEED CHAMPION- CHROME
HOOF- SKREAM- BENGA- GONG-
YELLOW MAGIC ORCHESTRA-
DIE! DIE! DIE!- ERRORS-
DROP THE LIME- DALEK-
SKEPTA- JME- AFRIKAN BOY-
ESAU MWAMWAYA- GAY AGAINST
YOU- SECRET CHIEFS 3- ZU-
VARIOUS PRODUCTION- FLEET
FOXES- DANDY WARHOLS-
HEARTBREAK- + MANY MANY MORE

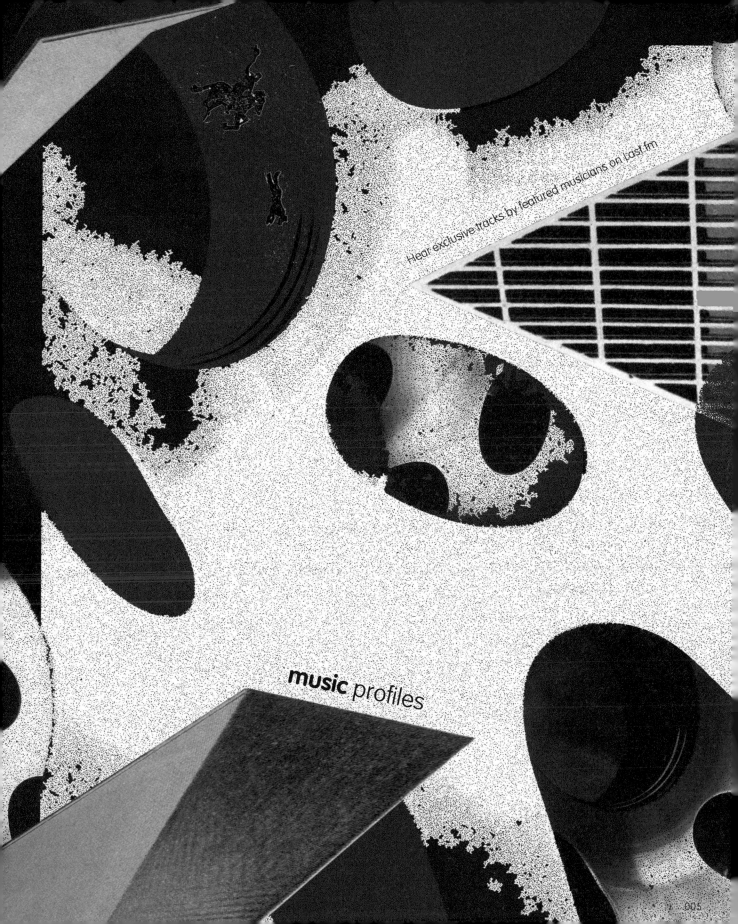

Hear exclusive tracks by featured musicians on Last.fm

music profiles

Alessi's Ark

Cursing the District line for only running one train every six hours, I reach the Virgin offices clammy with sweat. Alessi eschews a handshake for a hug as I wheeze my ever-so-professional hellos, and I fall a little bit in love with her straight away. Plus she looks like an ethereal woodland sprite, and in my book that is a charming look.

I get straight in there with some hard-hitting music questions... and ask which animals she would have on board her ark – it's always good to be prepared for a flood. Alessi's wish list runs as follows – one meercat, one ferret, two squirrels, one elephant (Indian), one manatee, one turtle, two snails and one praying mantis. I would pay good money to see this bizarre circus in a confined boat space.

Sadly, her chosen performing name does not come from a belief that Alessi is the reincarnation of one of the most memorable Old Testament characters, Noah. Rather it was born from a search for a name that didn't infringe on other Alessi named goods (including an identical-twin pop act from the 70's and an Italian kitchenware brand). "After many weekends spent with the whole family sitting around the kitchen table, thumbing through dictionaries and encyclopaedias in search of a good performing name, my mum finally thought of Alessi's Ark right out of the blue. And it was perfect. I wanted a name that reflected the adventure my music career is going to be for me, as well as for all those people who will help me. It's like my friends and family are all on board to help me make decisions and we're sailing along this career path together," she explains.

Signed to her label the day before her seventeenth birthday, Alessi is quite the protégé. Not content with singing, songwriting and drumming (she's been tapping out beats since she was eleven), Alessi also dabbles in illustration: she designed the artwork for her first and second EPs, and is currently collaborating with her nearest and dearest for the artwork on her upcoming album.

Unsurprisingly, Britain's education system could not contain Alessi's ravenous creativity. "Although I did enjoy school, I always felt like I wanted to have something outside homework to busy myself with in my free time," she says. Thus, when she was fourteen, Alessi's 'zine Brain Bulletin was born. This homemade 'zine was first distributed in a launderette in Shepherd's Bush. "I hoped that Brain Bulletin would fall into the hands of people who would like to contribute to it," she explains. Whether this was the right venue for such wishes is a little unclear.

But the two-dimensional world of magazines could not hold Alessi for long either. "I became more and more interested in learning the guitar and writing songs, and soon I was playing small gigs and just putting my music out there," she muses. Such was the reception that Alessi relocated to Omaha, Nebraska for six months in 2007, to record her EP under the direction of Mike Mogis, guitarist for Bright Eyes. Despite the public perception of the mid-west as a cultural vacuum, the time spent in Omaha proved integral to Alessi's growth, both musically and emotionally. "It's a real hub for artists and the people of Omaha are the most genuine and kind I've ever met," she expands. "So I found a like-minded community... and their pumpkin patches are awesome."

When asked about her influences, Alessi acknowledges a particular love for male singers. "I don't know what it is that makes me feel more affected by men when they sing," she sighs. "I like the way that men tell their stories, and perhaps it's also because I like to hear how things are from the other side of the battlefield." More specifically, she loves veteran singer Graham Nash and well-established indie bands Built To Spill (from Idaho) and Neva Dinova, from you guessed it – Omaha.

Now that she is already halfway to conquering the world of music, I want to know what else Alessi would like to do with her life. Looking a little terrified by the idea (maybe late on a Thursday night is not the most conducive time for mulling over such heavy life questions) she takes a few moments to answer: "I would love to go into music therapy. A friend of mine works for a program in New York called Feel the Music! which helps children who have lost a parent in the 9/11 terrorist attacks and have communication issues due to that trauma to come to terms with their loss through music. That would be such a humbling job. I would love to help people." Alessi is indeed a rare find in the egocentric world of music.

By this time it's nearing midnight, and the high rise office space we're interviewing in is starting to creep us out (inexplicable noises echo down the cavernous corridors) so we hightail it out of there; I return to darkest Peckham and Alessi goes back to her woodland.

The Horse EP is out now on Virgin and an album will be out next year

MySpace: alessisark

words | Catherine McColl
photography | Julieta Sans

"I actually wanted to have a shop here," fifty percent of Psapp, Galia Durant, tells me as she ushers me through the Shoreditch entrance to their world. "I thought it'd be really good but you need a license, which seemed a hassle, and Carim was like 'do we really want people coming in and out all the time?!'" Instead, artfully scattered toys and knicknacks on an oversize desk create a kaleidoscopic world of colour – a three dimensional mish-mash as effortlessly inventive as Psapp's trademark melodic electronica.

For the photoshoot Galia insists on straddling Carim Clasmann, the other half of Psapp. They make an odd couple these two – he with his greying hair and homegrown tomatoes: "Our favourite colour – Fun Red," he explains as he hands me one to devour. As the juice explodes everywhere I suddenly see Psapp's Fun Red all around me; in Galia's skirt and in her chunky round beads, in the curtains and on at least two of her fingernails.

Galia and Carim didn't warm to each other immediately. "In fact the first few sessions we did together were not that amazing," says Galia, "but there was obviously some connection because we persevered and gradually everyone else (we were working with) fell by the wayside." She breaks into a laugh of genuine bewilderment. "There's just something between us and it works! I don't know why; it's all a bit crazy."

I can really sense the ease between the two, who could easily pass for a couple. "When we write stuff together it's as if we're one person," explains Galia. "So it's funny when people ask 'what do you do in the band?' I mean, okay, obviously I do most of the singing, but I don't do all of it." Carim is similarly most likely to play guitar, but not always. They don't have set roles, or indeed methods of working. "We always start with nothing," says Carim enigmatically. "We don't use a template, or a formula, or any chord structure. We think it's nice to come from any angle possible." Conversation cuts over to Galia.

words } Paul Hanford
photography * Jenny Lewis

"Sometimes we're like extensions of each other. We're like an octopus, with all these extra hands! And there's so many things we don't have to say to each other; we can just communicate through our own sign language. I think that together we're more than the sum of our parts. On our own we're just horrible, pointless wastes of space!"

Galia writes most of the lyrics, and I wonder if she ever gets possessive about their content. "A bit, yes, but I try not to. If you're working with somebody else you have to accept their input, and unfortunately that means letting go of things you may think are good if the other person doesn't. That's what creates a genuine and equal partnership."

The Camel's Back is Psapp's third album, and as on previous releases it features copious use of obscure instruments such as the humble kazoo. We move to the rear of the building where their studio is located, and I am treated to the kazoo duet that features on new track Parker. I tell them that playing kazoo hurts my lips, and they kindly offer me their wooden kazoo to try out as an alternative. "There is a kazoo for any occasion," determines Carim, "my favourite is our special vintage kazoo which has to be played through a two-foot cardboard tube and is partly dampened by a cloth." Parker has a distinctively Charleston-esque flavour. "Recently we've been listening to quite a lot of New Orleans jazz from the 20's," Carim confesses. "There's so much good music from the past that there's no need to try desperately to like any new band that comes along. Good music is good music, and it doesn't really matter if it was made one hundred years ago or yesterday."

Both are keen on the juxtaposition of objects which have found their way into the wrong environment, hence an abundance of boats in sand, headless cats and suitcases at sea in album artwork. With The Camel's Back, Galia confesses that there were a few problems. "My camels all look as if they are trying a bit too hard to be trendy so they become a bit soulless." Whilst all artwork is a joint project, Galia is actually responsible for its realisation. She has also made a cult success of another creative endeavour – at her Craft Night in west London punters are given craft materials and encouraged to create a little something as they listen to a few carefully chosen bands. Galia's favourite recent experience involved a catering oven and some Shrinky Dinks. "There is something about molten plastic, drunkenness and miniature objects that really works," she explains. "Making sock puppets whilst having a rave worked really well too." Galia's dad, who was instrumental in teaching her the art of songwriting, plays a starring role at Craft Night. "He makes beat poetry that references Dadaism and 30's comics. I am not sure whether everyone appreciates the sophistication of his raps but even if they don't, he has a wonderful beard to look at."

One of Psapp's songs was recently used in the cult American TV series Grey's Anatomy, a fact of which Galia is not that proud. "Part of me says 'I just don't care, who fucking cares?' So. We did some songs and then someone approached us and offered us a load of money to play our totally unrelated song on their program." But she is obviously not that comfortable with the idea of selling out, whatever bills there are to pay. "I've watched a bit of it but I haven't even seen a whole episode. It doesn't interest me... and Carim doesn't even own a TV." But he does own some very fine kazoos, and I for one know which is more exciting.

The album The Camel's Back is out now on Domino

www.psapp.net

La Roux is a headstrong young lady – that much is apparent as soon as she materialises. Dressed head to toe in all manner of patterns, she exclaims that "my sister says I look like vom!" As in puke... "I like looking like vom though." As we head for a café she takes me on a mini tour of Brixton, the area in which she has grown up. She seems completely at home as we traverse the bustling and colourful local markets.

La Roux is Elly Jackson. Together with producer Ben Langmaid she makes electronica that leans towards disco; a lush sound that harks back to the heyday of 80's pop, awash with carefully-sculptured synths and intelligent lyrics. A frequent theme is personal experience in love, and how it "makes you lose your sight."

Was music a big part of your education? Music wasn't a part of my education at all. I hated music at school. I hated the way it was taught. But it was good in primary school cos we had this teacher who would do really fun things with us. She would write her own political songs and once a week we'd have a big singalong where she would give us all something to hit or play along with. Then once I got to secondary school everything started to get really, really formulaic. So I just ignored everything I got taught. They would give you a book and tell you to read a page about Mozart, and then make you answer questions about him. That's just not music. I am much better at learning on my own.

Were there any other musical influences during your youth? My parents would play me really good old skool music from an early age, and my father started to teach me guitar when I was six, which was a big help. We'd listen to lots of folk and rock 'n' roll, stuff like Buddy Holly and Bo Diddley. I wrote my first proper song when I was about thirteen and played it to the family. They were like, "that's really good for a thirteen year old!"

I heard you were discovered at a party. What happened? Well, a few years ago there was a forty-eight hour New Year's party at The Prince [a pub in the centre of Brixton], and it was about four in the morning. I was sitting in a little room upstairs, just messing about on a guitar, in my own little world. Turns out somebody was listening and went off to call their friend who was a producer – which is how I was introduced to Ben, the guy I am now working with.

So how did working on the album develop from there? After speaking on the phone I went to Ben's house and we started talking about my influences. I played a couple of songs to him that he loved, and we started to meet once or twice a week. We worked on acoustic tracks for about a year and a half because the backing tracks were never quite right. I guess it feels very natural for me to play on a guitar, and it felt weird to move away from it. Eventually I clicked with the synthesizer, and then we had

La Roux

to take a break because we didn't have any money! But when I came back to Ben and said "Look, I've written this song on a synthesizer and I love it. This is the way forward," he was like, "That's so weird, I've just made this tune that's really electro with an old friend of mine, and I was about to come and tell you this is what we should do!"

How do you think people respond to your music? Essentially I make pop music, and I want people to respond to it in the same way that you might instantly get up and dance along to the Eurythmics' Sweet Dreams in a club, even if it is pure pop. 80's acts like Yazoo, Depeche Mode, Eurythmics and George Michael wrote really great melodies with lyrics that you could really relate to, which nobody seems to do anymore, and it's those tunes that I look back to for inspiration.

How long has it taken to record the album? It's taken about three years... but then Ben always said from the get go that it was going to take at least two years to do. Stuff likes this always does. It hasn't bothered me though cos I didn't want to rush anything; I just wanted to make a really good record. It took until about this time last year to properly hone our sound and since then everything has really come together.

What tends to spark ideas in your songwriting? Ben and I write the lyrics together and although it's great working with someone – we sometimes come up with the same line at the same time – we're usually quite frustrated and emotional about it. A lot of the time a title will just come up in conversation and we'll write a song around that. Once we've sat down with an idea for a song we can't leave it until it's done – I'm always gagging to sing the lyrics and start work on the backing track.

You haven't played any of these songs out yet. How do you want the live show to work? I want it to be a really different experience – a spectacle, more of a show. I don't really want it to be just two people playing keyboards. I know to begin with it's going to have to be quite small, but I'd like it to grow into something more extravagant.

What is it like to be involved in the music industry so young? To start with it was weird because my friends and family have such a negative view of the industry and at first they didn't trust any of the people that I am working with. But I think that I have managed to persuade them that at the end of the day I have a working partnership with my label and if I want to be a success I have to help them to do it well. When my parents actually met some of the folks at my record company they were shocked at how nice they were, and I was like "I know, of course they are! I wouldn't work with them otherwise." Mind you, my friends are definitely weirded out that I'm doing interviews and photoshoots.

Both full of falafel and fruit juice we bid each other goodbye. Elly steps into the street to hail a taxi home, trailing in her wake an enormous bag of clothes brought along for the shoot.

The single Quicksand is out in December on Kitsune
and a debut album is due for release early next year

www.laroux.co.uk
www.kitsune.fr

words } Charles Drakeford
photography } Retts Wood

Simon

words } Dearbhaile Kitt
photography * Brendan Peer

Bookish

What's in a name? It's a question etymologists have pondered over for years, and a question I now ponder whilst waiting for Simon Bookish, who has been caught in the London traffic. Specifically, I am wondering whether Simon Bookish is actually bookish by nature? When Simon arrives, apologizing on behalf of Transport for London, he reveals at my prompting that not only does he like a good read but that he also has a part time job in a library! Furthermore, once I am back at Amelia's HQ a quick google of the meaning of the name Simon reveals that it means To Listen. So, what's in a name? In the case of Simon Bookish, a heck of a lot!

Simon Bookish is the pseudonym of classical composer Leo Chadburn. Leo trained at the Guildhall School of Music and Drama, and his recent work has included sound-art installations, improvisations with the bands Leafcutter and Polar Bear, electronic scores for the Royal Opera House and compositions for the National Theatre. As Simon Bookish, an English eccentric singer in the best meaning of the tradition, he has released three albums, of which Everything/Everything is his most recent. I wonder, does Leo end with classical and Simon begin with pop music? And does it ever get difficult to juggle a split personality? "I don't feel like I wear my classical musician jacket anymore. Most musicians take inspiration from other sources. Even the classic rock band who doesn't play anything written after 1960 is boring. I don't want to hear a rock band that doesn't know that dance music exists and vice versa." Well, that's a relief then; no need to keep the two endeavours separate.

The cover artwork for Everything/Everything pictures the bespectacled Simon in a garishly patterned blazer sitting behind a desk, news-reader style. Laid out on the desk are periodic symbols and on the wall behind is a world map, apparently depicted covered in black smog. So, what's the album about? "Science, information, art and history." Fans of romance will be disappointed, for the lyrics are designed to be intellectually engaging rather than emotional: not that Simon is immune to feelings – he confesses that he felt a bit lonely with only his "orchestra in a laptop" for company and decided to include his friends on this album.

On Everything/Everything almost every conceivable instrument makes an appearance in his quest for "a big band sound", marking a departure from the previous two synth-heavy albums. One unexpected instrument that gets a look in is the recorder, and it transpires that Simon has had a long affinity with this most simple of instruments, having opted to study "early music" during his degree. "To play the recorder well is as difficult as any wood instrument, maybe even harder!" I confess that I find it hard to take the recorder seriously, but he reminds me that it actually has its own place in a full orchestra. As I start to say "I used to play..." Simon cuts in to relate an anecdote from his days at the Guildhall. "My tutors were as serious about the recorder as any concert violinist is about the violin, but every day they would have to put up with somebody saying 'the recorder! I used to play the recorder at school!'" I'm rather glad I don't get to finish my sentence.

Unlike me, Simon's first foray into music wasn't with the recorder, but with the oboe and clarinet at the age of eight. These days Simon dabbles in "a little bit of all instruments, but I don't really play anything anymore." Now that his classical training is behind him he's "not interested anymore in having immense technical skill in any one instrument." Instead, he is more interested in the timbres and structures of music and has chosen to wield his voice on this album, perhaps born from a need to a be an all-composing all-singing jukebox. "It's really easy to write something straight away and then perform that piece without waiting for others to help out. The voice is a really portable form of expression."

We are nearing the end of the interview, but still one niggling question remains. Who is this book lover's favourite author? "I love the way that Thomas Becket forms his novels, using repetition and the unfolding of emotion in a structured way. I think his methods can be easily applied to music." So, what's next for Mr. Bookish? "I'm easily bored and at heart I'm a modernist, so I'm always doing a combination of things and I try not to repeat myself. I'd like to do something theatrical, and I also want to work on some really quiet acoustic music. The point is that nothing ever stays the same: if a formula works give yourself a pat on the back and move on." And no doubt this musical maestro will.

The album Everything/Everything is out now on Tomlab Records

www.simonbookish.com
www.tomlab.com

"I really wasn't expecting this. I was told I was gonna be on the dole or working in a shit job and not earning any money." You might think from twenty one year old Mica Levi's grateful outburst that I am treating her to an interview at the Ritz, but we are actually sitting outside a greasy spoon caff just down the road from the Guildhall, the music college where she is a student. It's Mica's choice of location, having bypassed a much trendier coffee shop that deals in organic lattes and Wi-Fi, in favour of cheery red and white signage and the prospect of two teas for little more than a quid.

Of course Mica isn't just grateful for the tea, her outburst is actually referring to the quite frankly astounding reception that her band, Micachu and The Shapes, have been getting of late. The band is made up of Mica, performing under her stage name of Micachu, on vocals, guitar, and electronics, along with keyboardist Raisa Khan and percussionist Marc Pell. With Pure Groove record store bigging them up as 'the toast of London town' and a BBC Newsbeat headline asking 'Is Micachu the next big thing?' it's a wonder it isn't all going to her head. "All that stuff's very nice but I don't really know about it that much. It's probably healthy for me to stay away from it. It's just hype, isn't it?"

Micachu has come a long way since I first saw her playing her distinctive brand of experimental electronic pop with only a little tape player for company over a year ago. "I spent a year going around playing really, really small gigs and open mic things. It was a pretty horrific experience cos you're on stage by yourself and you feel like a bit of an idiot." She describes that time quite negatively, which is unusual for such a positive person whose 'yeahs' often come in fours.

It was this, and Mica's desire to have a different live sound to her recorded stuff, that led her to seek out fellow students to join her as The Shapes. Just talking about the duo makes Mica's face light up and she is back to being positive. "The Shapes? Yeah, they're great. Really down to earth. They're both very good musicians and really interesting producers. Yeah, yeah. Really, really happy with the band so, yeah, best move I've made so far."

With increased press interest and a bulging MySpace calender that betrays a very hectic schedule (the band seem to have a gig on every night as they gear up to the release of their debut album, Jewellery), I wonder if her band mates knew what they were getting themselves into? "No, and I don't think I really did either. It is fun, but there are elements of it which aren't. It's not necessarily that creative actually, being in a band. There are a lot of things like waiting round and... interviews. No offense!" she laughs. "But, it's quite a weird thing to do; just constantly to be reflecting on what you're doing as opposed to just doing it. But you can't complain, obviously. We're very happy."

It's strange to think that, with all the gigs and media buzz, Mica is still a student. It must be even weirder for Mica herself,

a thought that is confirmed when she admits she hadn't wanted to be interviewed at her college for fear that other students might think she is "up herself". The fact that Mica studies composition and has had one of her pieces performed by the London Philharmonic Orchestra shouldn't seem as strange as it does, considering she has played violin and viola since the age of four. But her music is defiantly left of centre and her Filthy Friends mix tape is undeniably grimey so I have to admit that I find her classical leanings a little unexpected...

"I think you'd be surprised by how many electronica producers have had contact with studying an instrument, even if it was just playing the piano or something when they were younger," she comments sensibly. "My study is centred on twentieth century western classical music but I'm very open minded."

When I ask about influences, Mica screws her face up, her head obviously filling with a million names. She eventually picks out rapper Big L "at the moment one of my favourites for his wit," the blues musician Otis Rush, Captain Beefheart "I'm not really into prog rock but I like that he's a bit mad," and avant garde composer George Antheil. "At the moment I'm interested in music that is clear in what it's doing, and really honest with it. Like grime, because it's really bold and it feels strong."

Harry Partch, an American composer who made his own instruments, also makes it onto Micachu's list of influences. Following in Partch's footsteps, Mica is herself getting into the realm of home-made instruments and, on stage, she and The Shapes will pull out all manner of strange accoutrements to make fresh and innovative sounds; beating everything from wine bottles to boxes with drumsticks, shoving pieces of card into fret boards and singing into vacuum cleaners to create distorted vocals.

"We're quite into our gimmicks. I think coming from studying all this experimental music, it doesn't even seem weird to us. It's just meant to be a bit of fun, really. With the hoover I can make myself sound possessed! It's quite funny. But it upstages us every time."

One last thing. Every time I've seen the trio perform they have always worn the same white t-shirts. Decorated with brightly coloured graphic shapes, they have become a sort of on-stage uniform. So, with a gig nearly every night, do the t-shirts ever get washed? "No. I probably shouldn't tell you that but no, very rarely. I've got two though, the rest have one each. We really need to make some more ..."

And that's about the level of star treatment Mica seems happiest with, two t-shirts instead of one. Oh, and to be bought a cheap cup of tea in return for an interview. It's clear that Mica hasn't let any of the hype surrounding her and the band go to her head, so there's no chance of her becoming a diva just yet..

words } Sarah Barnes
photography * Will Sanders

Micachu
& the shapes

The debut album Jewellery is due for release in early 2009
MySpace: micayomusic

words } Matt Bramford
photography * Retts Wood

PAUL HAWKINS & THEE AWKWARD SILENCES

Cacophonous antifolk band Paul Hawkins And Thee Awkward Silences are performing tonight in Kilburn, and I can't tell if their apparent nerves are due to this impending gig or the fact that I turn up looking less than presentable from last night. We take a seat...

So, what's the story so far?
Paul: I'd been playing guitar in my room for years and I needed a way to get out and meet people after I'd finished university and moved to London. By 2005 I'd recorded a demo, I was gigging regularly and then Ian emailed me...
Ian: (interrupting) I read a review and found him on MySpace – he'd posted a message saying that he was looking for someone to help arrange, erm...
Paul: Strings!
Ian: Yeah, so I messaged him about that and we ended up gigging and recording together. I'm actually a guitar player, but I didn't fancy that, so I volunteered as the drummer, so that was that.
Paul: Ian produced the album, which was a pretty small scale affair. Our collaboration was only ever meant to be a one-off thing.

So why Thee Awkward Silences?
Paul: We're not really sure but we like it. It's suggestive, and a lot of our songs are about communication on some level so it feels appropriate. I went through hundreds of band names, from Cactus 75 to Death By Chocolate, and One Sick Puppy, but as soon as I thought of this I knew it was the right one.

How do you fill an Awkward Silence?
Paul: Erm.......

Are Awkward Silences ever a good thing?
Paul: I think that they're fascinating because people don't like silences very much. There's always such an interesting relationship dynamic going on. All silences are awkward, right? But whenever you get a moment of absolute silence, then that's really amazing.
Ian: It's a bit like the performance piece, 4'33, written by John Cage, where he sits in awkward silence instead of playing music. The 'music' is different every time due to background noise. People paid to go and listen to that!

On MySpace, there's 907, 461 alternative bands...
Paul: Yeah, it's difficult. I think we're a bit different to everything else, but then all bands claim that they're 'different'. Sometimes I wonder if I am just deluded as well, but luckily most reviewers seem to agree. I think that people get us, but – you're right, there's no real word that's suitable...

Does the album, We Are Not Other People, pay a nod to this too?
Paul: Whenever my dad would deny me something that I wanted when I was a kid – like a microwave or a holiday to Disneyland – I'd say "but other people have got one" and he'd always reply "well, We Are Not Other People". It was his answer to everything and I hated it back then, but as I've got older, I find I understand that response better.

Have you enjoyed putting the album together?
Paul: Yeah, it gave me a massive buzz to finish it and I'm really proud of it. It can take fifteen attempts to record a guitar piece that's vaguely usable so the actual recording process itself can be a bit arduous, and it's doing well so it looks like we'll break even, which is the main aim! But in terms of immediate rush, nothing compares to being on stage!

What kind of gigs do you prefer to play?
Paul: We love playing at the Antifolk Festival, which is held at the 12 Bar Club in Soho. Some of our best gigs have been there; it's such a lovely small, intimate venue which is always full of people. It's pure unadulterated good fun.

What bands do you listen to?
Paul: Well, when it comes down to it, we basically appreciate pop music that is slightly kind of, erm, Ian – what's the word? Flawed?
Ian: Yeah. Jesus And Mary Chain are one of my favourite bands because they made pure pop music with an element of horror.
Paul: And I'm a big Nick Cave fan, which is probably apparent in our music; and I also like Belle & Sebastian and Elliott Smith, which might be less apparent. I am drawn to direct, open lyrics, which is what I also like to create.

What is your guilty pleasure?
Paul: Well, I was saying only the other day that The Communards' Don't Leave Me This Way is my favourite song of all time, but I don't feel guilty about it!
Ian: Oh, you mean a song?!
Paul giggles as I explain to Ian that yes, I meant a song, and am not interested in what he feels guilty about in his private life. Or am I?
Ian: Mine is Sailing By, which is a fifty year old piece of music that is played before the shipping forecast every night on Radio 4

Can you explain the philosophy behind songs like Don't Be Afraid Of Love?
Paul: I was actually aiming to write an 80's style power ballad, and I'm a bit disappointed that songs like Don't Be Afraid Of Love are perceived as cynical, even though they might be... a little bit... But they aren't a joke; those songs are very personal and I am genuinely interested in communication.

So what does the future hold?
Paul: We're going to stick together as a band and we might record an anthemic hymn. I'm not religious, but I'm hoping to do it with a full-on choir!

The album We Are Not Other People is out now on Jezus Factory Records

www.silenceisawkward.com
www.jezusfactory.com

The DandyLionesses

words } Catherine McLaughlin
photography * Olivia Kachman

As I wait for my cue to go onstage and recite the monologue I wrote as my part of Power Of The Land, I watch Susan and The DandyLionesses play in front of a barrage of inspiring images that were shot on farm visits across Grande Prairie, Alberta, Canada, where we live. They form a backdrop to a show that seeks to tell a wider audience about the challenges faced by local farmers .

The stories that we heard as we tramped across fields and inspected livestock were familiar ones: Susan was raised on a family farm near tiny Fort Assiniboine. At the end of each visit Susan would ask the farmer a favour: would they dance for her, for her camera? And every time, despite their reservations, they would agree. The images now accompany her song The Dream (and can be viewed on YouTube: Dancing In The Peace Country). A family dances in their field; a small blonde child skips in her red boots; an elderly bee keeper begins to twirl as she gleefully removes her jacket.

A recurring theme in Susan's music is our yearning for a connection with nature, family and community. For her MA thesis, Negotiating The Distance, she wrote an album of songs backed up with text, the first 'musical thesis' ever submitted at the University of Calgary. In it she pleads for us to let the land be our educator. With her band The Dandylionesses she performs at teachers' conventions across the province, entertaining and educating with songs from her thesis. In an introduction to I Fell In Love, Susan explains: "Borders are the places where we meet. The work is not getting over the borders; the work is negotiating them so that perhaps we have a larger space that we can all belong in."

Two weeks at Schumacher College in Devon this summer were life-changing for Susan. "It's the first place I've been where as an academic, a musician and a farm kid I felt that I belonged. I finally felt integrated as a person," she says. Susan's sister Christine, who also sings with her, tells me that "it's a gift to be part of a band that performs meaningful songs about stuff that matters: the sustainability of families, women, the environment. We are women's voices unafraid of kicking political ass, weeping with those who suffer, yet also joyfully embracing the fullness of life." Bass player Angie says that "Susan is an idea-factory and her massive dreams spearhead all sorts of performance concepts, bringing together eclectic performers in a way that touches an audience and often brings them to tears." We saw those tears after the Power Of The Land show when we joined the audience for food donated by farmers' market vendors, transformed by a local chef into delicious appetizers: local folk were at last noticed and appreciated for their part in our lives.

Susan has been weaving hands and hearts for years. Violence against women was the theme of the four annual Hearts Journey shows about "heartache, hell raising and healing" that she produced to raise money for our women's shelter. "Susan's passion through song reaches out to people and embraces them," affirms Wendy, the newest member of the band.

Organising Women In The Park in the summer and Womansong in late winter is Susan's way of extending a hand to other women singer-songwriters in the region, and designing original shows for their Peace Country audience is a deliberate choice of The Dandylionesses. "We don't tour; we don't leave our families," Susan explains. "We are mothers. We need to be really creative and find ways to make music in a small community, to foster in the community the value of what we do. But I'd be lost without all those people who think our ideas are worth supporting." And those people could well be lost without her to guide them.

LONELY

words | Katie Webster
photography | Jenny Lewis

GHOSTS

Amidst the dawdling ducks and doting mothers gazing into their prams on this bland autumn afternoon, I spot the fluorescent blue-jacketed Tom Denney (aka Mr. Lonely Ghosts) cautiously approaching the lake in Victoria Park.

I throw a silly wave as an offering to identify myself and soon feel regret revealed in blushed cheeks. As the threat of small talk dawns on me I suggest that we grab a coffee, and in a bid to avoid a conversation about the weather, I cut straight to the chase on an issue that's been bugging me. Is he lonely? Or a fan of the paranormal? It turns out that Tom's moniker was inspired by a far simpler love – of the concept of invisibility as a super power – powered by a lifetime obsession with cartoons and comics.

Formerly vocalist and co-guitarist of the now defunct but much loved indie band Help! She Can't Swim – a vexed, frantic and somewhat noisy affair, Tom is a pensive and slightly timid character. In his new guise this twenty six year old is more interested in "moving inward," writing lyrics about "working out who you are, where you are in the world and where you're going." Having grown up, courtesy of his dad, on a musical diet of Pet Shop Boys and Elton John, Tom aspires to make perfect pop. "Any kid who denies that Michael Jackson's Bad is genius is lying!" But he is content to be labelled an "avant pop experimentalist," confirming that his musical outpourings are a mash-up of influences, from his humble pop beginnings to a stint during the 90's listening to emo and hardcore.

Tom's first album as Lonely Ghosts is titled Don't Get Lost Or Hurt, which is what his Dad would say to him before he went outside to play. The artwork for the record, which he did himself, depicts a wounded child who brims with "quiet optimism." Some of the material was written during the dying gasps of his former band, begetting the kind of honesty that has culminated in "the closest to a love song I'll ever write. I've always wanted to make lush romantic songs with lots of texture, rather than simple love songs." More interested in the way that a piece of music makes him feel than the actual sounds used to create a song, Tom plucks out the "righteous and empowering" elements from bands like The Thermals or Bruce Springsteen as inspiration. His dream gig would probably involve a support slot for Bruce Springsteen but "any gig is good to get, and I don't mind supporting other people because there's less pressure that way." One of his favourite gigs to date was in the box room of a house party with accompaniment from an iPod.

Tom proudly tells me that he works from his home recording studio on a very tight budget, and his eyes light up when he reveals an intense moment on eBay which landed him with his "secret weapon," a bargain £40 synth. He neither has nor wants "unnecessary and extravagant tools." Apart from the occasional glass of red wine to get the creative juices flowing, there is no exact formula that Tom follows when writing. "I don't have much of a songwriting brain so I'll start with a few ideas on my keyboard or guitar and throw stuff at a song until it sounds right."

To determine whether a song is finished or not Tom uses a novel method: he bravely plays the uncompleted songs live to see what kind of reception they get. Despite officially being a solo artist Tom still prefers to play out with a crew, and often enlists former band mates and friends to join him on stage. I like the idea of different members of Lonely Ghosts floating on and off, a kind of ghostly foil to Tom's lonely solo status.

Tom describes the music industry as "fad based" but laughs that "there's only one of me so I can't really split up!" With a follow-up album already scheduled for release early next year and plans to tour with friends Munch Munch, The Tumbledown Estate and Pseudo Nippon (if they can all fit in a van) this man is surely busy enough. But when Tom is not working at the local cinema, making mix tapes or eating sushi he is also part of Brighton collective One Inch Badge Records, who have just released his album. Like so many others who have opted for the DIY route, this talented chap has his fingers in many creative pies.

The mini-album Don't Get Lost Or Hurt is out now and a debut album will be released in early 2009, both on OIB Records

MySpace: lonelyghosts
www.oibrecords.com

I first saw the North Sea Radio Orchestra at the Green Man Festival last year, in a wet field with a cup of hot, spicy cider; surrounded by indie-kids, flower children, families, rockers, anti-folk bands, the lot. Combining the unmistakeable sounds of a chamber orchestra with poetry set to swirling choral arrangements, this rambling collective have managed to create something altogether enchanting. I caught up with founder Craig "a lanky, lazy, moody man, but not without wit or charm." His words not mine.

How did the North Sea Radio Orchestra come to be?
My wife Sharron and I were in a band called Shrubbies, but eventually we got fed up with playing to bars full of noisy people on the toilet circuit. The audience were inevitably more intent on drinking and catching up on their social lives than listening to us, so we decided to form a quieter band that people would have to sit down to listen to! Thus the North Sea Radio Orchestra was born.

How did you come up with the name?
When Sharron was little she used to go to sleep to the sound of the North Sea crashing onto the beach. One night she fancied she could hear the strains of beautiful music coming from out to sea, but what she could actually hear was the echo of the North Sea Radio Orchestra rehearsing on an old Humber Keel barge on its way to London – destination St Martins in the Fields, where twenty years later we would make our debut. It's true!

What kind of music has influenced NSRO?
I don't really listen to 'proper' folk music very much but I love folky types like Joni Mitchell, the Dufay Collective, Neil Young, Elliot Smith, Vetiver, Ali Farka Touré, Sufjan Stevens and Bonny Prince Billy. Individual compositions that I love include Dirty Boy by Cardiacs, Peter Grimes by Britten, The Lark Ascending by Vaughan Williams, Drowning Witch by Frank Zappa, and California by Joni Mitchell.

What music informed your childhood?
I grew up in the Oxfordshire countryside before moving to Kingston when I was nine. The first record I bought when we moved to town was ABBA's Arrival. I think it was from this that I got my love of a good middle eight. My father would play classical music that would sneak up through the cracks in the floorboards into my bedroom as I was going to sleep. I remember the warm glow that I used to feel, almost a physical reaction to the music. I think that because I was half asleep the music entered my subconscious. I listened to a lot of pop during the 70's on my transistor radio; then I got into metal and prog rock. For a while I was only into 'complicated' music.

Poetry is integral to NSRO. How did that happen?
I have an innate confidence when composing, but with words I am on shakier ground; I do write lyrics but always worry they are no good. I love poems, particularly those of a philosophical nature, so I keep a few anthologies about the house, and sometimes I will read a poem and instantly know that I can make a piece of music with it.

Would you agree that NSRO makes very 'English' music?
Yes I would agree and I'm very happy when people say that. I live in the Wiltshire countryside near the ghosts of many long dead Britons: Romans, Saxons, Druids... But there are good technical reasons why my music sounds so English. There was an English Pastoral School of composers in the 20th century who shared similar approaches to harmony and use of traditional folk song and I sang a lot of this music in my very good school choir. I wouldn't compare myself to the genius of Britten or Elgar but I am a small part of that tradition – and I want to move it away from the classical scene and introduce it to new audiences. We get everyone from indie fans to OAPs at our concerts.

What are your current plans?
Our second album Birds – a mix of songs, instrumentals, choral pieces and miniatures – is out soon. It has a really strong atmosphere, much sharper than our first album. I love working with such a great group of wonderful, talented mentalists so I hope we can continue to grow, sell records and do special one-off shows. I want to make an emotional connection with the audience in whatever way we can.

Why are your fellow musicians mentalists?
What I mean is that they are all quite strong individuals, with their own unique oddities and flaws. As well as being excellent musicians they're very open with themselves and their opinions, and I like people who aren't defensive or secretive. This binds us all together and makes us a 'band' as opposed to a lot of chamber ensembles where musicianship is the only importance. I love working with them because they're generally good despite being a little fucked up – and in my experience all the best people are!

The album Birds is out now on Oof Records

MySpace: northsearadioorchestra
www.oofrecords.co.uk

North Sea Radio

Orchestra

words Sophie Hill
photography   Bohdan Cap

ILINA ORLOVA

word] Emma Hamshare
photography * Paul Paper

The Hoxton Bar and Grill is a hive of commotion as sound engineers scuttle between speaker stacks trailing tangles of wire behind them. The diminutive flame-haired Alina Orlova sits in the midst of all this activity, eyes closed as she tinkles on a keyboard and tests her unexpectedly tremendous voice. "My answers won't be good at all!" she laughs as she sits down to talk with me a few moments later. But she is soon chatting away in her charming Lithuanian accent.

School days

I don't really remember how everything started. I learnt piano and classical music at school and started to write songs when I was thirteen, but it was all funny stuff because I was so young. I met Simas [her violinist] when I was at school and we played during lessons in the school hall. I really wanted a record player but I didn't get one until I was older. So there I was, just a girl who loved music in a little town with no music at all to listen to.

Confused influences

I guess what I play now can be called folk… or something like that. I try not to classify my style because music shouldn't need to be named. I don't think I can say anything smart about my influences – I'm not professional enough to answer this question! But I guess I am very emotional, and there were many very beautiful forests and lakes around my home town so maybe that has influenced my style, but I never really think about it… and I've never listened to someone else's music and thought, 'that's what I want to do'. I just write some poetry and sit at the piano and start to sing.

Studio or live?

Well, I love playing live because you can feel the audience's reactions. And it is exciting to know that anything can happen. I find it scary but at the same time it's almost like I'm making a connection with something higher. In the studio I have to sit and think so it's not the same. But at least you can record the same song many times and correct it if it goes wrong.

The next album

I'm really excited because we're planning a new album at the moment. I love that feeling of waiting for something to come and not knowing what it will be like. Will I even like it? I always doubt everything, so sometimes I will dislike my songs even though it feels as though I am making something very important at the time.

Writing songs

Lithuania is a good place to write sad songs; when I was young nothing ever happened, so I had a lot of time on my hands and I would make up tunes and play them on my own. Now I compose the lyrics for a song before I come into rehearsal and when I start to sing and search for a melody the guys [in the band] will play what they think fits. But lyrics are not the most important thing to me; they are secondary to the more basic emotions formed by sounds.

Which language?

Once the melody for a song becomes clear I will know which language I want to sing it in because all languages sound so different. Russian is hard and sharp like a knife, so it can hurt. Lithuanian is much softer… and I can use really silly words in English and it will still sound good. I don't write many songs in English because I can't speak it so well.

Current release Laukinis Šuo Dingo features Alina's trademark haunting songs, sparsely scored against fairground-esque keyboards. Being an accomplished visual artist Alina has a hand in all her album artwork, and the cover of this features an illustrated mammal of indiscernible nature sat upon her elfin-like shoulder. Whether sung in Lithuanian, Russian or English, Alina touches those emotions that go beyond language or dialect.

The album The Wild Dog Dingo will be released on Metro Music in spring 2009

www.alinaorlovamusic.com

words } Charles Drakeford
photography * Retts Wood

DAS WANDERLUST

Folk-punk band Das Wanderlust are positively bouncing with energy, despite having been cooped up in the tour van for four hours. After they drop off all their equipment at tonight's venue, we head to a café across the road, where we sit as far away as we can from the noisy coffee machine.

At first glance Das Wanderlust look a little mismatched. Singer Laura is cute as a button, dressed like a 50's doll with a big smile to match her cheeky character, and guitarist Andy is incredibly warm and friendly, replicated in the casual manner he holds himself. But Wes, the band's drummer, seems a little aloof; dressed to the nines in a foreboding black suit. He's the most shy and retiring band member, although perhaps he is just playing it cool.

Das Wanderlust have already seen numerous line-ups despite their short existence, with even Laura getting confused by the situation. "I went to Goldsmiths [art college], but then I dropped out and moved back in with my mum and dad up north where I started writing loads of songs. A friend of mine knew a girl who played bass, so then I asked her to join my band... and that was Andy's ex girlfriend." Such frequent changes have helped to evolve Das Wanderlust's unique sound. "Quite a few of our old drummers couldn't play drums, which helped to contribute to a 'different' sound! Then Wes joined, who was a famous jazz drummer in the 1960s, well, in his head at least." Wes was first and foremost a fan. "He was like, 'Can I join your band please? I think you're so amazing. I'm so in love with your band,'" Laura relates gleefully, "and we said, 'Okay then!' and that's how we finally got this line-up together." Wes coincidentally (or maybe not) happens to be the owner of Don't Tell Clare records, who released Das Wanderlust's first single.

All these reincarnations have become something of a joke to the current band members. "Laura's mum is a prize winning marzipan modeller, so she was going to make a series of cakes, each bearing the marzipan grave of a band member who is no more," says Andy, "but we didn't do it in the end – we couldn't even decide on who we would class as ex-members!"

Their producer, Phil Davies – erstwhile drummer with Stockton band The Chapman Family – has been very central to the album recording process. "We don't record in studios because we're tight arses, plus we get all panicked, so instead we record in bedrooms and living rooms. Phil works for the very well known," Laura adopts a posh accent, "British Broadcasting Corporation, and he gets loads of microphones from..." Andy cuts Laura off mid sentence, before affirming that "we're just lucky to have a producer who can borrow good microphones. He's got a really good portable home studio, and he's a proper sound geek. Even though I used to be a sound engineer I have no idea what he's talking about

sometimes." Despite his worries about getting their producer into trouble Andy then goes on to say that Phil has been known to borrow dozens of microphones from the BBC, and that is just to mike up the drums. "He records hundreds of audio tracks for every song and he then wades through them to find the all best bits." He refuses to discard any old takes just in case he can make use of them. "Phil's a bit mental in that respect," laughs Andy.

The band's hectic tour schedule isn't much fun at the moment. "We're playing to a lot of empty rooms," says Laura. "It's still better than having a day job though." The problem, it seems, is that they have been booked to play in a lot of student towns during the holidays. They often share the bill with a local band, and the audience is invariably full of their friends. "We meet a lot of bands who aren't that cool, but when they're on stage they adopt this really cool attitude." In contrast Das Wanderlust act much the same onstage as they do offstage. "So we tend to insult each other a lot, and sometimes we even have arguments on stage," admits Andy.

Laura and Andy bicker constantly during the interview, but always in a good natured fashion. "I faff about between songs, and that annoys Laura. So sometimes she starts singing without me. Then I'll have to stop her because I'm not ready. Last night she called me a snail, which got me really annoyed." Laura just shrugs and laughs. "What can I say? He's annoying!"

Andy explains that Das Wanderlust make "wrong pop". "People always ask us what type of music we make and it's really hard to explain what we do. We don't make rock or punk, or anything massively avant garde or experimental. We just try to write pop songs but they always seem to come out a bit wonky."

The band create all their own artwork and produce and direct their own music videos – the video for the single Puzzle stars Laura's ten year old sister dressed up as a very convincing ghoul. In the video she befriends another ghost who met an equally sticky end, with one having been eaten by a shark and the other struck by lightning. "We try not to make anything look too slick or professional, but then we don't want it to look amateur or crap either," explains Andy. "Essentially we just like to be in control."

Das Wanderlust are one of those rare things – an utterly genuine and endearing band who are determined to do things their own way. By choosing to forego any professional razmatazz they have been successful in creating a delightfully individual entity. Catch them at a full venue soon.

The debut album Horses For Courses will be out in early 2009 on Don't Tell Clare

www.daswanderlust.co.uk
www.donttellclare.co.uk

SPORTSDAY MEGAPHONE

words } Charles Drakeford
photography * Julieta Sans

Sportsday Megaphone is the most recent project conceived by the multi-talented Hugh Frost, who spent his teens – like so many others who grew up in the 90's – playing in hardcore bands and generally making as much noise as possible in his friends' garages. When these bands inevitably went their separate ways Hugh, despite being happy in his work as a graphic designer, found himself at a bit of a loose end. "I missed making music even though I was really into my design work. And it felt weird to try and find people to play with when I had always played with friends, so I just decided to do it all on my own."

Hugh was exposed to all kinds of music growing up, thanks in no small part to the influence of his dad. "He used to have a habit, usually after a bottle of wine, of turning the stereo up really loud late at night and playing classical music until it shook the house," he says. "It was really dramatic, so I guess that was kind of instilled in me." His current sound has developed according to what has been readily available to him. "Keyboards are cheap; I usually pick them up at car boot sales," he explains of his synth sound. "It wasn't within my means to make a really smooth R & B or pop album!" So how easy has it been to take his music from the bedroom to the stage? "Most of my live show is premeditated: a lot of it is prerecorded – although that's something I would like to change in the future – and then I just add stuff to it. I like to put a lot of personal energy into the performance." Hugh freely admits that he's "not technically that proficient with any of the instruments", which is something I find endearing more than anything. I like to think of him as a modern one-man band, whose arms have been freed up by the use of laptops and samplers.

Hugh's music has a lot more heart than the usual run-of-the-mill bleepy music that is churned out by bedroom producers. He writes about parts of his life that anyone can relate to; in Less And Less he talks about his insecurities around strangers, and I Think It's Love is about chatting rubbish to girls to try and impress them. Not that he needs to, for nowadays he works with his girlfriend under the moniker OWLS, making music videos for the likes of Friendly Fires and The Maccabees. He has also done countless remixes. I wonder what his views are on the the state of the music industry today. "I don't understand why things that I think are important are not seen that way by others," he says in an exasperated tone. "Take music videos for example: there are more and more outlets available to distribute them, yet budgets for making good music videos are going down and down, which doesn't make any sense to me! That's just one thing that is messed up in the industry."

Hugh's talents outside music allow him to have a hand in almost all the other aspects that go alongside his album. In effect, he still has a day job: "I'm a freelance graphic designer, so I'm kind of just keeping afloat with my music and a bit of design. It's not bringing in loads of money, but it's enough to live on. Now the album is done though, I kind of want to get back to working on my design stuff for a little bit." As a designer, does he visualise the artwork when writing the music? "At first the only visuals that I could associate with the music were from iTunes or GarageBand or Logic, which are all really ugly programs. It's nice to finally have some artwork and an image that's specific to it."

Hugh is somewhat bewildered by the way his life is currently panning out. "It's weird. When everything is so music-focused and I'm playing gigs and talking about it all the time it's like I'm not really living and soaking things in." I get the sense that this album was a labour of love, and very hard to produce on his own. "I really want the next album to be the collaboration that this one should have been. I'm glad I've had the experience, but it was two years of stressing out, and there is a bunch of people that I really want to work with."

Hugh downs his orange juice so that we can start the photoshoot, during which he's not shy to offer up some ideas. He may be a long way off commercial success but at least Hugh is doing what he enjoys, doing it his own way, and producing some eminently listenable electronica to boot.

The debut album So Many Colours / So Little Time is out now and the single Meet Me In The Middle is out in December, both on Sunday Best

thecocknbullkid

words } Charles Drakeford, photography * Jenny Lewis.

I am welcomed into Anita Blay's house with a cup of tea on a comfy sofa, the soft exclamations of daytime TV reassuring in the background. I could easily forget there was a job to do were not the photo shoot already underway. Anita is certainly in her element, happy to showcase some of her many outfits. It's time to decipher the truth behind thecocknbullkid.

Where did you grow up?
I grew up in Hackney, with a brief stint in Walthamstow. Which coincided nicely with my East 17 obsession.

So when did you start getting into music?
When I was young I entered loads of dance competitions; I thought I was Vernie from Eternal! With my friends I had a band dedicated to Eternal and we even had a white member as well. I started writing music when I was about eight and I would get my brother on the keyboards – we thought we were 2 Unlimited – and then we would bore my dad. Those bands were a huge influence on me – all the greats...

When are you going to release an album?
Well, although there is some interest in me I'm not signed yet, and I think it's important that I get the album recorded [if not released] before I make a commitment to anyone. I just feel I'll be in a much better position, and I don't want to jinx anything before then. At the moment things are just flowing along quite naturally because all my songs are still at the demo stage.

What inspires you to write?
The music that influences me most is just great pop music. Like Kate Bush, David Bowie, M.I.A. or Madonna and even Morrissey. When I hear amazing music it makes me want to write great stuff. And when I hear shit music it inspires me to make better songs too. I tend mainly to write about the bad times in life; about vices and taboo subjects that aren't usually talked about in songs. If I feel really down I find that the best way to deal with it is to write some music. Which I guess is quite healthy compared to some of the other things I could do! I'm quite happy at the minute and I'm still writing – which I wasn't able to do before, so I'm getting better at finding a healthy balance.

Do you work with anyone else?
When I first started out everything was self produced and it was very hard for me to accept help from anyone because I was so adamant that I knew what I was doing. But it has been such an eye opener to start writing with other people, because I honestly don't think I'd be able to make the sort of pop music that I'm making now on my own. It's relatively easy to make something experimental because you can just play whatever you want, but it's far harder to craft a really good pop song and I had to find the right people to help me do that.

I was really worried that I might end up making disposable pop, but my producers are very aware that everything I do needs to sound like thecocknbullkid.

How else do you like to be creative?
I'm not really into fashion but I find it really fun to throw things together and see how they look. I love jackets, bags, shoes... and wigs. Those are my things!

You seem to be getting some much bigger shows now, and you've had loads of festival dates this summer. How do they compare to smaller venues?
It's much easier to play at a bigger venue because you tend to have more space to move around and you feel more important. And there are fewer people literally right in front of you with their eyes boring into you – it can be a real challenge to play at a small venue.

How long have you been performing with a band?
For about a year and a half it was just me and a backing track. That was all I knew when I started. I hadn't ever played with other people before and I really didn't know what I was missing until I started playing with the band! But eventually I got bored of singing along to the same backing track; there's no dynamics, nobody to bounce off. Performing with a band improves everything by about ten fold. It looks better and the sound is so much bigger.

I heard that you were planning to collaborate with Metronomy ages ago. Is it ever likely to happen?
When I first met Joe about three years ago we decided to work together because we both just really liked each other's music. It was going to be a side project called Anita and Joe... but neither of us has had the time... maybe one day! It's definitely on the cards.

I leave Anita's Hackney flat safe in the knowledge that I've unearthed at least a few truths about the girl behind the moniker thecocknbullkid. Having decided that the fabulous world of melody holds far more appeal than the reality of urban life, she's working hard to set the dancefloor alight. The eight year old Anita would be well impressed.

The single On My Own is out now
and a debut album will be out early next year

MySpace: thecocknbullkid

BRIGHTBLACK MORNING LIGHT
Motion To Rejoin
Matador

This album plays like a session in singer Naybob Shineywater's smoke-filled tepee; nuances jostling amongst the layers of Rhodes synth; moods and melodies seeping into the sunset. Honesty is abundant in the lyrics but sometimes the music fails to carry this sentiment. The record seems unsettled: sounding languid yet unsettling; reactionary yet complacent; concerned with the greater good yet self-serving; hopeful yet mawkish. As a result the album is what Timothy Leary might've referred to as metastable. What is consistent, however, is the sound attained by Brightblack Morning Light – a warm, woody, sort of sequestered psych-folk mantra, steadily drifting along. The music is suspended comfortably between soul and ambient, with vocals that echo wistfully throughout. For all the slightly bashful moments, considering lyrics especially, there are also moments of melodic inspiration where the elements of psychelic rock shine through – the outcome of which is an instantly more credible record. However, whilst kow-towing to the powers of Sativa, Brightblack Morning Light have failed to realise that the respect for nature held by autochthonous peoples is born out of survival instinct; not a fanciful, opt-out camping trip à la City Slickers II: The Legend of Curly's Gold. Posturing aside, at least the album is "aligned with the phases of the sun" – its recording powered by solar energy. All is forgiven. **FK**

AVALON
Labyrinth
Every Conversation Records

As soon as I hear the name Avalon, a deep-rooted memory of the Roxy Music album of the same name is awoken. Avalon the band couldn't differ more from the dapper croon-fest that was Bryan Ferry's masterpiece. They are a group of sprightly boys from Tokyo who have a lot in common with Late Of The Pier, largely in the way that they take a very futuristic approach to pop music. Saying that, they're not afraid of resorting to classic techniques, with the use of church organs on Andromeda Saint Chime suggesting something a little more menacing than the shiny pop featured elsewhere. It's one of my favourite points on the album, but the award for best track must go to Evil Loves Devil with an intro that evokes memories of old Sega Mega Drive soundtracks, only for it to descend into glitchy, rattling guitars. It is Avalon's approach that defines their style more than a specific sound; focus rapidly shifts between instruments, with everything from cowbells to organs thrown into the mix. This has the effect of leaving my head spinning, unsure of exactly what I've been listening to – but certain that I've enjoyed it. There's no doubt that Avalon have been heavily influenced by of-the-moment acts Justice and Klaxons, but this album showcases a healthy dose of originality too. **CD**

HEADLESS HEROES
The Silence Of Love
Names Records

American singer-songwriter Alela Diane fronts this stunning collection of covers, pulled together by Eddie Bezalel after he discovered her unique voice on MySpace. Spanning a period of forty years, the aim was to rediscover little-known classics and reinterpret them for a new audience, so expect songs written by a diverse selection of artists. The album opens with True Love Will Find You In The End by Daniel Johnston; a heart-breakingly beautiful paean to the complex search for true love, "Only if you're looking will it find you / Cos true love is searching too." Tackling the iconic Vashti Bunyan on Here Before is a brave act indeed, but Alela's crystal vocals perfectly suit the tinkling production. Just Like Honey by Jesus And Mary Chain is probably one of the better known tracks on the album, and it has to be said that Alela sings it with considerably more clarity. Nick Cave & The Bad Seeds are also ripe for reappraisal on Nobody's Baby Now, which uses the echoing production typical of this album to beautiful effect. With many of the original tunes likely to be unfamiliar to people, this record stands out as a unique piece of work in its own right, and will no doubt help to cement Alela's rightful place in the pantheon of great folk singers. **AG**

Album Reviews

FRANKLIN
Lost House
Wool Recordings

Franck Rabeyrolles is best known for recording minimal French folk electronica under the name Double U, but the Lost House EP sees him deliver a slice of neatly arranged and dreamy indiepop under the moniker Franklin. Lead single Lost House is the closest we get to the electronica of old; a warm analogue synthesiser bobs up and down under electric cymbal swells and blips, over which Frank croons in a suitably francophone style. But Into The Dark is even better; all textured reverb, plinky xylophone and delicately produced psychedelic delay harmonies, Yo La Tengo meets Icelandic superstars Múm. Why wasn't the CD named after this song, I find myself asking? Big Cities cleverly plays with off-kilter beats in a painfully beautiful ode to our inseparable bonds with urban culture. If you like intelligent, relaxed and lushly harmonic electronica with a heart, then this is for you. **PG**

ESSIE JAIN
The Inbetween
The Leaf Label

After an astonishing debut release London-born New York-based folkster Essie Jain returns with an impeccible, stimulating second album. With simple, haunting melodies that are stripped to the basics this is Bat For Lashes sans bells and whistles. The usual synonyms apply: fragile, tender, arresting, intimate; but this album is definitely not one for the emotionally unstable as Jain's unforgiving lyrics and orphic melodies tap directly into the psyche. Less is definitely more on this romp through the emotions, with piano, strings and brass accompanying Jain's enigmatic vocals. Undoubted highlights Eavesdrop, Please and Stop pack the most punch, and there is an evident increase in confidence in the experimental The Inbetween, which is destined to become a modern classic in the world of all things folk. This is no album for wild parties, but with all its poetic sadness and heartfelt vocals it is a must for those who revel in thought-provoking, enchanting refrains. **MB**

MIA VIGAR
True Adventures Happen Inside Your Head
Hungry Audio

Mia Vigar has left behind her Luma Lane guise to present the listening public with her first own-name album. Sitting in that delightful subdivision of pop inhabited by the likes of Bjork and Kate Bush, Mia seeks to create her own beguiling reality through her songmanship, with vocals veering from a softly worded feline whisper to a punky, urgent screech. At times she verges dangerously close to a recent phenomenon displayed by pop musicians: the self–consciously Estuary school of singing (hands up Kate Nash et al), but thankfully Vigar's energetic, slightly crazed delivery makes comparisons with Satomi Matsuzaki of Deerhoof more apt. The album is constantly surprising, stuttering and jerking its way from haunting piano pop, to spacey instrumentals, to fast paced hand-clapping melodies. All of these are infused with a naivety, the kind of eerie childlike sound reminiscent of an antiquated jack-in-the-box. Hesitantly played recorders and unsophisticated keyboard sounds further emphasise this sense of nostalgia, while Vigar's manipulation of birdcalls, drone-like bells and other evocative samples contribute to the dense atmosphere. True Adventures Happen Inside Your Head is a perfectly chosen name for an album that beautifully weaves a unique world through the minds of its listeners. **BR**

HOLLYWOOD, MON AMOUR
Hollywood, Mon Amour
The Perfect Kiss

Those readers who remember the 1980's no doubt got down and dirty to Prince, Duran Duran, Survivor and Simple Minds. If you didn't – what were you doing? Drinking Cherry Coke and sucking on Pacers whilst playing Pac-Man? But I digress, because those hits are back by way of a Parisian jazz bar. Inspired by seminal Hollywood movie soundtracks, Marc Collin (one half of Nouvelle Vague) has reworked all the classics with the help of a few chanteuses. Juliette Lewis, Skye from Morcheeba, Cibelle and rising star Yael Naim all lend vocals to the tracks, which are stripped of their overblown synthesizers to become French lounge-sophisticated. Breaking ranks, Call Me features a wobble board that would make Rolf Harris smile and the familiar tring-tring of a bicycle bell introduces A View To A Kill, but having searched out the originals on YouTube, I have to say I prefer their overblown bluster. Covers are always a Risky Business (sorry!) so I applaud Collin's attempts to reinvent such loved hits, and for those more cosmopolitan moments this album is indeed perfect. Just don't expect anyone to jump onto their chair waving an air microphone. **DK**

DAWN LANDES
Dawn's Music
Boy Scout Recordings

This Kentucky-born New York-based musician specialises in quirky homemade boho folk of the type that on paper might sound irritating but on record is absolutely captivating. With a delicate voice that belies a subtle intensity, Dawn sings against a backdrop of scuzzy guitars, glockenspiels, softly tinkling triangles and crashing melodeons. Unafraid of experimentation, she often leaves in the detritus of recording; spontaneous asides "that should be enough of that part", chuckles and in the case of Honey Bee, sniffles. The plodding drumbeat of opening tune Suspicion perfectly echoes the sentiments – a dogmatic desire for "faith in me". Mud & Stars tells the story of differing points of view, with a much fuller sound intimating the possibility of giving in to strong emotions. Twinkling flutes and answering accordions spiral in a melodic dance in standout instrumental Traffic. The result is a sparkling intimacy that'll have you tapping your feet in no time: Dawn is one talented songstress and this is one purchase I urge you to make. **LB**

LOYAL TROOPER
One Day All This Will Work Out
Self Released

For anyone who's been stuck in the ghost world specially reserved for twenty somethings wondering what to do with their lives, Loyal Trooper's new EP One Day All This Will Work Out will prove particularly poignant. The Trooper himself, singer-songwriter Andy Walker, sums up this peculiar period in six guitar driven tunes which tell tales of vacuous peers, dull desk jobs and the gentrification of a once loved home town. You might think with such subjects at hand the whole atmosphere of the EP would be pretty maudlin but, whilst the lyrics may be dripping with cynicism, the melodies are surprisingly upbeat. Chirpy first track Nottingham Wasn't Built For Me will leave you itching to get up and dance like a loon with your dearest friends. It's important to register that Loyal Trooper is most definitely, and defiantly, Northern. For starters, the name Loyal Trooper is a tribute to Walker's favourite pub in his home town of Sheffield. As a fellow north-erner, I can relate to Walker's stories of a wide eyed graduate who has moved to the capital only to find the pavements are more grey than they are golden. Stand out track M1 To The A52 rounds off the EP in a much quieter, acoustic vein. This is a reassuring collection of songs that lets you know that you are not alone because no one really knows what they want to be when they grow up. **SB**

LARKIN GRIMM
Parplar
Young God Records

Straight from Devendra Banhart's school of kooky anti-folk, Memphis-born Larkin Grimm is unnaturally gifted. The multi-instru-mentation on her third record Parplar is constantly impressive, and there's a dark heart beating behind the cage of stringed tools she builds around her voice. Dominican Rum is stunning, displaying a sound instilled by growing up with singers and fid-dlers in the foothills of the North American Appalachian Mountains. There's spirituality in many of her songs; and Be My Host's references to unicorns and the Holy Ghost sound natural, not try hard. She's as at one with ideas outside her own as someone raised in a creative community should be, but the soaking up of influences is also the record's weakness. Sporadic descents into minute-and-a-half long spazz-outs go nowhere and wind up grating. Parplar's best moments come when Grimm de-cides to splurge her experimental creativity all over the place (check the title track). Her sound is wholesome and earthy, so it's fascinating to hear it countered with artificial bleeps. On Durge she sings in a foreign tongue, adding to the mystery and wonder of the record. Larkin is way more interesting than the usual hippies found clinging to Devendra's knitted coat tails. **TH**

NEVA DINOVA
You May Already Be Dreaming
Saddle Creek

This well-produced third offering from Nebraskan favourites Neva Dinova begins with a deceptively dreamy aura. A smoky-voiced Jake Bellows croons through opening ballads Love From Below and Will The Ladies Send You Flowers. The obscurely named Tryptophan, named after an essential amino acid, is an ode to hopelessness. From here on in the tempo picks up, with What You Want featuring excitable Oasis-esque guitar riffs, swiftly followed by the short but haunting Funeral Home, chock full of multiple harmonies and coming in at just 1:18. It's Hard To Love You is a winner, featuring a singalong melody and acoustic guitars against a wall of sound. The influence of grunge is unmistakable, so if you're still yearning af-ter the golden days of Nirvana this album is the perfect antidote to the commercial guitar pop so common nowadays. **TP**

OLLI COLLINS
Counting Electric Sheep
Eleven Recordings

It's always difficult to replicate the sweat and energy of a nightclub on a rather clinical 1.1mm thick compact disc, and this di-chotomy is probably at its most extreme when it comes to house, electronica and drum 'n' bass records. Olli Collins' debut offer-ing of funk inspired house is no different; attempting to mix the oddly gritty experimentation of a kid who has just discovered his all-singing, all-dancing keyboard with the professionalism of a well respected DJ on the London circuit. First track Rain stands out as an ironic sun-kissed sub-bass track better suited to an Ibiza Chillout compilation but the album as a whole is a pretty varied rucksack, from the clashing rock tinged Killers to the freaky electric futurism of Dreamseeker – which sounds like the soundtrack to some twisted 3000AD sci-fi film. Counting Electric Sheep claims to be '12 sonic blasts' and over the course of fifty five minutes it's a fine example of how to mongrelise multiple genres into one complete progressive house album. For maximum effect, only air after twilight hours. **JD**

NIGEL OF BERMONDSEY
Nigel Of Bermondsey
Pure Mint Recordings

This is the first solo effort from Nigel Hoyle, ex-bassist of now defunct Brit pop band Gay Dad, and it's a rather heartfelt affair. Think Lemon Jelly style wistfulness mixed with esoteric psychedelia breezily sung in a faint falsetto. The first single off the album, Overload, has all the charisma and sheen that British pop music seemed to project with such ease during the 90's. Many of the songs carry infectious melodies that wrap lyrics around lovely little guitar riffs, but there is a part of me that wishes there had been less glossy production on the record. With such strong songwriting there's just no need for so much instrumental layering, which occasionally detracts from the tracks. But for a first solo effort this album is hard to fault and deserves a place in your CD rack even if you weren't or maybe because you were, a fan of Gay Dad. **CD**

REMEMBER REMEMBER
Remember Remember
Rock Action

Signed to Mogwai's Rock Action label, the debut album from Glasgow's Remember Remember is a beguiling listen. You find yourself in a rich, occasionally playful atmosphere built on complex, loop-based arrangements with the sort of unusually sourced percussion (bubble-wrap, hole-punches and Irn-Bru all make an appearance) that you would have associated with Martin Hannett in his lunatic prime. There are simple piano arpeggios in opener And The Demon Said, guitar lines reminiscent of Another Green World-era Brian Eno in Genie along with Afro-beat style guitar chops in The Dancing and delicate glockenspiel and classically tinged violin in Fountain. It all combines to create a sound that is ambient but not monotonous, gentle and mellow but not wrist-slashingly dark, a kind of 21st century re-imagining of Durutti Column, only without Vini Reilly's occasionally dodgy vocals. Overall, quite an uplifting experience. **RP**

SQUAREPUSHER
Just A Souvenir
Warp Records

Bassist Tom Jenkinson is a peculiar and prolific musical genius, but the idea of an entire album's worth of jazz freak-outs would usually have me running a mile for fear of being bored to death. However, Just A Souvenir is interesting, and I mean genuinely interesting – not just in a music geek kind of way. Combining his trademark electronica with jazz, Squarepusher has managed to retain the distinctive broken structures for which his oeuvre is best known. This concept is at its most innovative on The Coathanger, which features a totally infectious bassline that is echoed, elongated or bent into disarray leaving you eagerly anticipating its return. Undoubtedly there are tracks like A Real Woman which don't work as well, where the use of obscure, warped vocoder vocals is never going to warrant repeated listens, but on others he manages expertly to fast-forward elements of rock into the future in a truly inspired way. It's a far cry from his earlier work, and at least a thousand times more mature than My Red Hot Car, but there's no danger of Squarepusher hanging up his bass just yet. **CD**

THE BOAT PEOPLE
Chandeliers
Ivy League Music

Yay! It's The Boat People. Who? Well they're Australian, and they kind of sound like The Shins, but not really, and Chandeliers is their second album, and it's pretty awesome. They sound like a band you know from somewhere deep in your memory, probably because even from the first listen you feel as if you could sing every word. Part of this is probably down to the fact that The Boat People incorporate many much-loved musical ideas from the past, all jumbled into something new. Mostly upbeat, at points Chandeliers runs the risk of becoming just a bit too happy and twee. I don't know what it says about me but it's the more introspective and melancholy tracks like Hours n Hours that really appeal to me. Overall, the casual familiarity of this album makes it a thoroughly enjoyable affair. The Boat People are not out to offend; they haven't got any kind of ulterior motive. They just make nicely written pop songs. **CD**

FRIDA HYVÖNEN
Silence Is Wild
Secretly Canadian

Silence Is Wild is an impressive album, both for Frida's songbird voice and her wonderfully simple yet evocative arrangements. With spellbinding power, her highly personal yet insightful lyrics sit astride simple piano and string accompaniments reminiscent of Regina Spektor. Drama is created in the most subtle of ways, with layered strings providing occasional orchestral depth, most notably on Enemy Within. Frida is from a small town in Sweden, a fact which informs her songwriting. Scandinavian Blonde is a rip-roaring send up of Scandinavian stereotypes and in My Cousin she relates the story of a cousin's marriage and plaintively asks "I'm not the marrying kind, and neither are you / But still I am absurd enough / To ask you, if we were the marrying kind / Would it be my hand you'd ask for?" Who this intimate song is addressed to is never voiced – an imaginary lover who she would like to father her kids. "Will you be the dad? / Other children I most likely won't have." This is a wonderfully original album which manages to avoid being overly saccharine through Frida's uniquely personal sentiments. **KW**

THOSE DANCING DAYS
In Our Space Hero Suits
Wichita

What happens to all those oh-so-very promising school bands? Those peculiarly gifted kids somehow exempt of regulations, flaunting their risqué hair and modified uniforms, invariably fancyable, doing covers of whatever is sort of cool that year at the local youth club, even the occasional assembly. Fast forward into the paunch of their thirties and most have unspectacularly fallen into McJobs and compromised relationships, ungainly clinging onto this brief moment of regional fame. This all-girl Swedish five-piece are still fresh out of school, but carrying all the enthusiasm of the common room they have produced a glimmering hit parade of pop gems with the kind of punch that you can expect from fellow country folk The Concretes. Standout track Shuffle is a cunning list of song titles culled from singer Linnea Jönsson's iPod, a gimmick that fortunately never sounds forced. In Our Space Hero Suits is an exuberant collection of playful pop that is destined to become a classic. I think a lifetime of disappointment will be spared. **PH**

words } Nat Miller and Sarah May
photography * Annie Collinge
bats • Nat Miller, set design ^ Sarah May
illustrations ~ Val Sarakitprija and Nat Miller

the blood bath bat ball r.s.v.p

midnight at hairs horrow

In the deepest, darkest cave resides two pondering and plump young bats, who are discussing their invitation to the Bloodbath Ball.

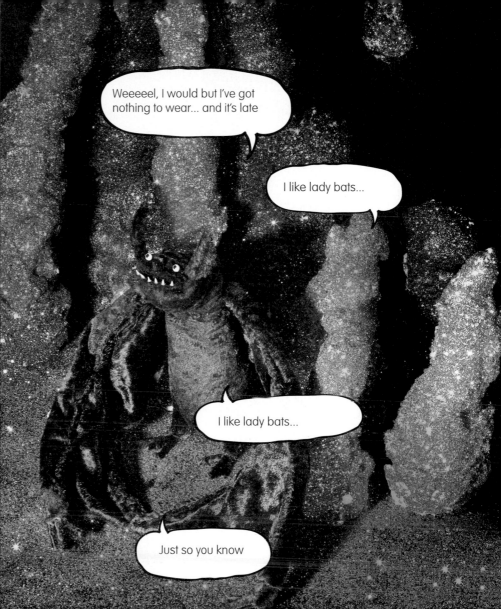

Fed up of his cave-mate moaning, Vinnie drags Bartrum out for a last minute fashion spree. Unfortunately these late flyers are out of luck for all the shops are closed.

Weary from their long fashion-hunting flight Vinnie and Bartrum rest their stocky legs on a near-by washing line. Swaying steadily on the twiney line, the two bats gradually loose hope of attending the Bloodbath Ball and meeting all the most eligible young lady bats.

Told you that you look good in anything – that top really hugs you in all the right places...

Thanks to Bartrum's quick thinking, Vinnie's previously untapped ability to sew and the missing articles of John-Jaque's wardrobe, the two bats quickly assemble the most outstanding outfits in double quick time.

So... whenever you find a sock or pair of tights missing from the line just remember the good cause it has gone to – and be grateful those little critters didn't take your pants!

Oh yes!

Okay! Let's go!

fashion & beauty profiles

Time is precious and timing is key. These truisms burn into the back of my mind as I sit on the sofa in People Tree's offices flicking through their new catalogue and making a mental shopping list. I am waiting to interview Safia Minney, the founder of the fair trade fashion label, and Bora Aksu, the fashion designer who has been collaborating with the brand for three seasons.

The timing of this interview couldn't have been any worse, with London Fashion Week just around the corner. Bora is preparing like mad for his own s/s 09 show, of course, but People Tree are also busy. Not only do they have a stall at the British Fashion Council exhibition to organise, but Safia also has her book, By Hand – The Fair Trade Fashion Agenda, to finalise for print.

Bora arrives, a little breathless, and soon Safia is free from her work so we move into the meeting space, a high ceilinged room with black hanging rails full of clothes lining each brick wall. Sitting down around a large oval table, Safia and Bora take the opportunity to run quickly through some plans for a future project. Although I had imagined the two would be stressed and weary, they are nothing of the sort, and chatter away eagerly. Their excited patter, interspersed with Safia's peals of laughter, brings to mind the relations of old friends rather than business associates. The smell of bacon rises up from the café below and, pushing away the niggling thought that I wish I'd made time for breakfast, I start by asking them how they got together.

PEOPLE

Safia: Together with Vogue Japan we identified some key designers that we really wanted to work with and when we sent a letter of invitation to Bora he responded very positively.

Bora: For the 2007 collaboration we only made one garment, but the response was really great so we went on to make a small collection. This a/w we've created a much bigger collection so we've really gone for it!

Safia: People Tree coming together with a very high profile designer was daunting; for instance I didn't know whether I would be able to ask for any changes to make a piece more saleable. But the lovely thing with Bora is that he is so open and doesn't have an ego, so we've built up a really good trust. We're still waiting for him to slap us around the face and shout "What have you done to my dress!?"

The two burst into laughter once more. However, it isn't all fun and games, and I soon learn that Safia is a woman on a mission to educate complacent fashion consumers. She talks often of fast fashion, likening the bland qualities of high street disposable garb to the un-nourishing aspects of a typical meal of burger and chips. With a determined glint in her eye she quickly pounces on my use of the term 'ethical' fashion.

Safia: 'Ethical' fashion could mean anything, so if a large mainstream factory which isn't fair trade uses organic cotton fibre they could be described as 'ethical'. The difference with People Tree projects is that they're all extremely small – we have lots of workshops in incredibly rural areas of Bangladesh and Nepal, where maybe forty people do everything by hand. We've really set the benchmark for best practice within the industry and we will keep driving our ideas forward because we want the industry to catch up. Child labour still exists, so there's a long way to go. The reality is that the industry is not even meeting the minimum requirements in terms of wages or health and safety.

Do the requirements of People Tree's manufacturing ethos mean that Bora has to modify the way in which he designs his distinctively tailored, feminine garments?

Bora: I don't think it effects the way I create but it does affect the technical side. The way I design is usually very generous in fabrics, but with People Tree I need to consider the restrictions of a hand-woven fabric that comes in a certain length, and adjust my design accordingly.

Safia: Have you ever felt creatively restricted by our collaboration?

Bora: I actually quite like the challenges because one of my design philosophies is based on the idea that if you restrict yourself the results can be much better. If you restrict your inspirations or your fabric...

Safia: You're forced to think outside the box!

Bora: Yeah! Also, I just love the process of creation with People Tree. When the garments come in I'm so amazed by how technically able the workers are. The results are such good quality that some of the factories in Italy would have a hard time competing. But that's because no one is doing this just for money's sake – everyone puts his or her heart into it, and it shows in the final garments.

Sophie wears drape dress by Bora Aksu for People Tree, top by People Tree, clown bowtie and shoes stylist's own

This extra care and attention is obvious in the current Bora Aksu for People Tree collection. The range sees aubergine pussy bow silk blouses with wide puff sleeves alongside olive organic cotton jersey tunics with flattering draped fronts. Safia is full of praise for Bora, noting his foresight that ensures everything he designs will be bang on trend once it hits the rails. Perhaps it's some sort of time machine, I suggest. "That's what it is! Take me with you next time!" Safia cries, playfully teasing Bora. So, I wonder, what does the future hold for their own collaboration?

Safia: We have to be careful not to overextend each other!
Bora: We both get very excited. We have meetings like this, I bring my ideas and Safia brings fabrics and details of what we can do and one thing leads to another and we end up with a whole rail of designs.
Safia: I can't wait to do something with you that's just completely out there. Something really embellished and gorgeous, it would be great to do that wouldn't it!? How about next collection?

And with that the two bid fond farewells, with Bora eager to get back to the preparations for his catwalk show, and Safia due in Japan the next day. I leave the dynamic duo, quite in awe of their seemingly endless enthusiasm. I can't wait to see what they will come up with next. I just hope they have the time...

words | Sarah Barnes
photography | Will Sanders
styling | Nadine Sanders
models | Marianne and Sophie Byron at Select
hair | and make-up | Shama at CLM using
Bumble & Bumble and MAC Pro

words } Dearbhaile Kitt
photography * Patrick Johansson
styling • Jennie Bramer at Muse Style Agency
models }{ Charlotte O and Max S at Avenue Modeller
hair ¶ and make-up * Emma Nilsso at Muse Style Agency
thanks to Carlsten Fortress

Laitinen

scarf by Laitinen, earring by Cornelia

Dolce & Gabbana, Viktor & Rolf, Antoni & Alison and erm, Marks & Spencer; fashion has always loved a double act. The Finnish siblings behind label Laitinen are the latest duo to emerge blinking onto the fashion stage, and despite having produced a mere four collections, they can already count Ann Demeulemeester as a fan. Tuomas and Anna Laitinen founded the label after winning first prize at the Hyères Festival, which, for twenty two years has been launching fashion careers from the unlikely setting of Provence. Tuomas tells us a bit more about their background and influences.

Can you explain your design process?
Both of us have been obsessed with fashion, art and other visual fields since we were kids and we're still collecting images, objects, fabrics and other stuff pretty much 24/7. Before we really start working on a collection all this random junk is brought together and we somehow make sense out of the puzzle by thinking of ways in which we can transform it into the kind of garments that we'd like to wear. That's the fun part really, after that it's pure hard work.

Do you design with a specific person in mind or is there a specific decade that influences you the most?
Well, it may sound egoistical, but the only people we think about whilst we are designing are ourselves. We have to be able to wear every single piece of the collection; otherwise we really can't call it ours. There are loads of people whose personal style we adore and whose work we respect, but we hate too obvious references and nowadays there's way too much homage paid to the past, in fashion anyway. We're terribly nostalgic and foolishly romantic, but we think that the result should always be modern.

Are there any recurring themes in your collections?
Every collection is a continuation of the previous one. We really want to stay true to our own aesthetics and develop the label slowly. We're really not into designers who do hippie for spring and grunge for winter. We don't really think about themes too much and sometimes our references are more obvious to other people than ourselves. I guess there's always something a bit melancholic and dark in our collections, probably due to our northern roots. Our clothes have been called moody, but we absolutely hate that word! It just doesn't reflect the sense of humour, tenderness or fragility that we feel is important in our work.

As brother and sister do you find it difficult to work together?
We're both a bit difficult, so I don't think anybody else could handle us! Some people tend to think that we're a bit intense, to put it mildly. But we find working together pretty easy, because it feels as if we are identical twins separated by five years. We often get the same ideas at the same time and our taste is almost identical. We're both very critical of our own work, so it's good to have someone else in the studio taking a more realistic view. We entered Hyères with our first ever joint project and then for the first two collections Anna did the knitwear and jersey while I was responsible for the tailored pieces. Nowadays we no longer have such strict roles so every item ends up having a piece of both of us in it.

How did winning at Hyères change things for you?
Hyères changed everything. The festival put us in contact with the best Italian fabric mills and introduced us to many of our current buyers. It's also quite amazing when you're just starting your career to have a chance to work with industry legends like casting director Maida Gregori-Boina and DJ Frederic Sanchez. It really hasn't been the smoothest of rides, but without Hyères it surely would've been even more difficult.

How did studying for an MA at Central Saint Martins compare to your previous studies in Helsinki?
St Martins creates its own universe, where you eat and breathe fashion. The place itself is completely rundown in comparison to the Finnish colleges with all their fancy equipment, but the extraordinary staff and students make the college the unique place it is, and million-euro laser-cutting machines cannot compete. It can be a very cruel place and the course director Louise Wilson really tears you into pieces to see how far you're willing to go with your creativity. But in the end it's all for your own good if you really want to work in this industry.

At what age did you develop a taste for fashion?
We've both been obsessed by fashion and images for as long as we can remember. Our mother was and still is a fashion freak with a fantastic wardrobe full of Comme Des Garçons, Martin Margiela and Yohji Yamamoto, so I guess she can be held responsible for our choice of career. She surrounded us with books and magazines from a very early age, on everything from literature and art to architecture and of course fashion.

What did you wear as children?
Like most Finnish or Swedish kids who grew up in the 70's and 80's we were dressed in Marimekko jerseys with crazy clashing stripes and polka dots in really bold colours. I still think Marimekko makes the best childrenswear. It was like Comme Des Garçons Tricot for midgets! I would wear it even now if they made it in my size.

What music do you listen to when designing?
We're awfully stuck in the past. Somehow all these new indie bands feel so manufactured and calculated. They're like cardboard copies of our old heroes Morrissey, The Cure, Pixies and Pulp. I know it's terribly clichéd for a fashion designer to say that he or she loves David Bowie and Patti Smith, but we honestly do. While we've been working on the next collection for s/s 09 it's mainly been the Jesus And Mary Chain on the stereo... and of course Courtney Love; she's the last true rock star in our books.

What other designers do you wear?
I have a massive Raf Simons collection because I have been buying his clothes continuously for more than ten years. When I look at it I see it as one continuous story not only of his career but also of myself growing up. Anna has a wardrobe full of Comme Des Garçons, but I know for a fact that she can't live without her over-the-knee Ann Demeulemeester platform boots. They're officially the coolest pair of shoes ever.

Would you say that people are more aware of ethical issues in Scandinavia?
We choose environmentally friendly yarns for our knitwear and we try to do most of our manufacturing in Finland, where more consideration is given to ethical issues... which means that our costs are close to astronomical when compared to the costs of manufacture in countries more used to mass production! For us the most ethical thing we can do is to produce a high quality product which can be worn from one season to the next.

sweater by Laitinen, necklace by Cornelia

words } Melinda Neunie
photography * Amy Gwatkin
styling • Alex Cunningham
assistance ^ Chloe Bell
retouching ^ Ben Crawford

AKAMUTI

Somewhere far away, hidden quietly in the deep valleys and serene rolling fields of Llansawel Wales, there is a long winding path. At the bottom of it there is a large detached house, and here live the Hedges; mother Anita, father Stephen and siblings Lindsey, Jennifer, Daniel and Karis.

Though this may sound like something out of a fairytale, this isolated farmhouse actually houses a thriving business. Twenty five year old Lindsey and her family ditched suburban England for the wilds of Wales back in 1997. "I've definitely adopted Wales as my home country!" laughs Lindsey. "I like being far away from the maddening crowd." She founded Akamuti – meaning Little Tree and A Little Bit Of Medicine in Zambian – in 2003, born out of a keen interest in herbal remedies. "I've always had a real passion for plants and tree medicines, so when I got to about nineteen I decided to blend them all together so I could make a living by doing something that I was passionate about."

Starting out alone in the farmhouse kitchen, Lindsey has since reeled the rest of the family on board. "It was natural to involve them as time went on. One by one the girls became involved, followed by the boys a few years later. Now everyone is working on it full time," she tells me.

While Lindsey works on the marketing and product recipes, the rest of the team use their individual skills to take on specific roles within the company. "My sister Jennifer helps me to come up with new recipes and products. Because she's so creative she also helps with design and writes the monthly newsletters. Then there's my mum Anita; she handles all the cream making. My dad is in charge of all of the bottling, soap cutting and accounting, and my little sister Karis is a bit of a whiz on the computer, so she helps out with that when she feels like it."

Last but not least is brother Daniel, who believes he holds a somewhat masculine position within the company, having the role of shea butter cutter and all. "Despite being a manly sort of man Daniel has a phobia of all things waspish," explains Lindsey, "so when the local wasp population decided to give their queen a guided tour of the workshop, Daniel bid a very noisy and hasty retreat into the ladies' office. He refused to return to work until the wasps had been evicted."

Sustainability is a key word in the family dictionary, so the Hedges do everything in their power to live a completely holistic lifestyle. "We eat organic, biodynamic and fair trade food as far as is possible and affordable... and we also attempt to grow a lot of our own food," says Lindsey. Father Steve tends to their prize plot of seasonal fruit and veg, whilst the rest of the family watch over the mountain sheep as they graze the farmland during the winter. In the summer the grass is tended to make organic meadow hay. But not content with merely leading the sustainable lifestyle at home, the Hedges have applied their ethos to their business. "For our skincare products we focus on the principles of tree, herbal and ayurvedic medicine, which use plants that work with our body's natural healing mechanisms."

Starting soley with Comfrey Balm, the Akamuti range has now grown to include herbal ointments and essential oils for aches and pains, alongside a variety of deliciously tactile jewel-coloured skincare goodies. It is Akamuti's bolder products that really stand out: rose-coloured Himalyan Salt Chunks the size of rough cut fudge pieces and candy-like Myrrh Gum resin – a powerful anti-bacterial agent – are beautifully presented in minimal paper packaging. "We want to convey the raw power of nature in its untamed form," says Lindsey, "so we try and retain the earthy soul of the ingredients by using them straight from nature as much as possible." This means lots of chunky slabs of shea butter, thick dark honey, golden beeswax and freshly pressed coconut oil. This ideology has reached its zenith with their innovative (some might say, as old skool as they come) whole soap nuts. Yes, this Indian nut, straight from the wondrous soap nut tree, really does clean your clothes and dishes on its own.

The Hedges relentlessly scour fair trade databases to source their ingredients, trying wherever possible to import directly from small producers in Africa and the Pacific. And with all the Hedges now involved in the Akamuti empire, they are able to handcraft at least two product lines a day from start to finish. "My favourite product is the Rose Facial Oil," beams Lindsey. "Its gorgeous heady scent always makes me feel better, so I carry a bottle wherever I go." With plans to expand the workshop and learn how to grow herbal ingredients in their very own aromatic garden Akamuti looks set to remain a very local family business – albeit far more than just a labour of love. For now, Lindsey leaves the pressures of work behind by curling up with a large glass of red wine on her favourite chair. Choosing not to travel due to its detrimental affects on the environment, she escapes on mini-adventures through books.

MARK LIU

I request to meet Mark Liu at quite possibly the most inconvenient time of the season: with only two weeks to go before the kick-off of London Fashion Week he is quite literally knee deep in fabric when I arrive at his studio in Islington. It takes a nervous cough to rouse the slightly frazzled figure before me, and only after a short walk to the local Thai take-out to pick up black bean noodles does Mark relax enough to answer my questions.

Born and raised in Australia, Mark Liu studied fashion and textiles at the University Of Technology in Sydney before accepting a place on the MA Design for Textiles Futures course at our very own Central Saint Martins. "I really like London because it's such a complete contrast to Australia," he tells me. "Because we are such a small population most of our clothing is a knock off of other peoples' designs. I really enjoy the fact that people love fashion so much here. If you try and describe it to people at home they just don't get it – the weather's too good, they just don't understand!" I wonder how his interest in design managed to develop in an environment so indifferent to fashion. "I went to this really obnoxious private school where everyone was destined to be a banker or lawyer but I was really into sculpture so I spent all my time drawing and making things. When I realised that there was no way I could get a job [in Australia] as a sculptor, I decided to express myself through fashion."

Unlike most graduates who leave University feeling very much poorer but no more prepared for the world of work then when they first started, Mark's MA course appears to have played a huge role in developing his first commercial collection. His debut Zero Waste range was launched in 2007 to industry acclaim, securing him stands at Climate Cool By Design, Fashion Conscious and London Fashion Week's prestigious Estethica exhibition, not to mention an appearance in the book Sustainable Fashion: Why Now? Immediately, he had a platform to show buyers his innovative pattern-cutting technique which attempts to reduce the amount of wastage accumulated during the traditional dressmaking process. "In western tailoring a minimum of 20% is automatically wasted," he explains. "So I attempt to hybridise western tailoring with eastern principles by basing all my patterns on rectangular shapes." To this end he has studied methods of efficiency optimisation and an obscure branch of applied mathematics known as 'game theory' in an attempt to generate the best waste-reducing pattern designs. I ask if these processes have limited his design ideas at all. "Sometimes I can't do exactly what I want," he says, "but because I am following a pre-ordained set of rules it becomes an art form. Like writing a sonnet – limits can give you new ideas."

Ashamed to admit to Mark that all this theory is making my head spin a little, I attempt to steer the conversation in another direction. This just leads to talk of another obscure concept that has inspired him, that of 'brinkmanship' – the practice of pushing a dangerous situation to the brink of disaster in order to gain the best outcome. "I like the idea that some things become more beautiful because they are dangerous," he explains. "For me the ultimate show of brinkmanship was to start my own label, so I just kind of went for it... it was quite reckless, but, now, here I am!"

Luckily, Mark's desire to skate on thin ice has resulted in the magnificent pleats and curiously patterned cutout kaleidoscope shapes of current collection On The Cutting Edge. "I can see my designs being worn at parties," he says. "They should be worn by someone who is willing to live a glamorous and slightly dangerous lifestyle; by someone who wants to stand out from the crowd." This wish seems somewhat at odds with his genuine passion for the future of our planet. But whilst his most forward thinking concept of Zero Waste pattern cutting has propelled him to the forefront of sustainable fashion Mark is admirably honest about how far he can go as a business just starting out. "I don't yet source ethical fabrics because I haven't been able to devote the right amount of time to proper research. I don't want just to pick up any old fabric because it has a stamp on it – but for my next project I am determined to research it properly."

Mark Liu is still a baby in the mammoth industry we call fashion, but with a host of awards under his belt and one foot already firmly wedged in the door, what are his plans for the future? "Just imagine how sophisticated my techniques will become within ten seasons," he beams. "and just think of what new ones I might be able to bring to the table. I have a whole book full of ideas that I want to test out." As Mark, ever vigilant to wastage, scrapes up the final morsels of his noodle lunch, I get the sneaky feeling that it won't be long before his itchy fingers set him back to work again.

Frankie wears dress by Mark Liu, lace top and gloves stylist's own
Francesca wears dress by Mark Liu, top stylist's own, gloves from Bang Bang

Jess wears dress by Mark Lui, lace top from Beyond Retro, hat by Noel Stewart

Frankie wears dress by Mark Liu, lace top and gloves stylist's own, tights by Tabio

words } Melinda Neunie
photography * Chiara Romagnoli at Wilde Hague
styling • Lilia Toncheva-O'Rourke
models }{ Francesca at Premier,
Frankie and Jess Findlay-Brown at Models 1
hair ¶ Nina Beckert at Soho Management
make-up ° Sharon Ive using MAC

Goats have taken a tough rap for long enough. Vilified in medieval times as a conduit for Satan, the common image of a devil still bears goat-like horns and a 'goatee' beard... and well, no one wants to be a scapegoat right? Now it's time for goats to officially buck their way up in the desirability stakes and this is thanks in no small part to Goldie, Myrrh, Botany, Snowy, Cirrus and Nimbus, who all live at the delightfully named Christmas Croft on the serene Moray coast of Aberdeenshire, Scotland. It is to here that art teacher Christine Ralph and her family uprooted when her over-worked London lifestyle became too much. Not for her the delights of a commute; instead she prefers to hand milk her goats, who together provide ten pints of glorious goat milk per day.

"In London the garden was my haven," Christine explains. But it wasn't enough: Christine hankered after more green space, so one fateful day the family packed their car with children, dogs, rabbits, lovebirds and a beehive. Knowing no one, they departed for the wilds of rural Scotland. "It was quite a culture shock to find that everyone you meet wants to know everything about you," laughs Christine. "In London such detailed questioning from a stranger would be considered a little forward, if not rude, but here it is the norm."

When the family inevitably began to acquire more animals they chose ones that would be well suited to their exposed position on a hillside, such as Highland Cattle, Jacob Sheep and a Shetland Pony. And then they were given three goats; the love affair had begun. "Goats are very useful creatures," Christine tells me. "Their milk is of excellent quality, they will graze land that other animals turn their noses up at, and they are companionable animals." But the newbie crofter had to find a use for all the extra milk she found herself with. "There really is a limit to how much goat's cheese you can feed your family," laughs Christine.

The Gamrie Goat soaps took a mere twenty three versions to perfect, but eventually Christine discovered that if you mix goat's milk with the best coconut oil, shea butter, caster oil, cocoa butter and olive oil it is possible to produce a truly luxurious chemical-free unscented soap that caters for the most sensitive of skins. "I recently decided to cut out the use of palm oil because it it is impossible to source it ethically; most of it is extracted from areas affected by deforestation. Instead I use almond oil, which is one of the best oils for moisturising the skin, and totally ethical." Christine won't use any added fragrances or colours because they can be irritants. "I get very dry, sore and itchy hands in the harsh Scottish climate and I know that I am not alone; many people with sensitive skin find it very difficult to find genuinely natural, effective products." And it only smells the tiniest bit goat-like in the end.

The soaps are as handmade as they come: twice a day Christine heads out to milk her happy gang in the barn. "Some goats like being milked, some don't, but there is a strict order in which they come out for milking and woe betide anyone who tries to vary it," she explains. "I put classical music on while I do the milking, and some of them, especially Snowy, visibly relax." The Gamrie Goat soaps are presented in lovingly hand-crafted recycled cardboard boxes, each bearing a photograph and profile of a particular goat. One lucky customer might learn, for example, that Goldie the goat is interested in politics, that Myrrh is a domestic goddess, or indeed, that Snowy likes classical music. I wonder if she could be guilty of anthropomorphising her animals. "It would be an insult to ascribe, for no reason, purely human qualities to my goats ," she says. "All descriptions are based on an individual's natural behaviour. For example, Botany, like most goats, seeks out rare and tasty plants to eat – but in her case she does this in a particularly delicate, choosy, Victorian Plant Hunter kind of way!"

Christine often finds herself daydreaming as she does the milking, and has been thrown across the floor more than once by Goldie. "She sometimes catches me out! I know it sounds unlikely, but she is very strong. The last time she did this I thumped against a wall, hit my head and woke up slumped on a heap of muck with stars dancing around my eyes." She was left holding a spilt jug of milk, and "rather pathetically began to sob." Until, that was, she thought of her mother wagging her finger and saying 'it's no use crying over spilt milk.' Which made her laugh instead.

Sunny, a male, has not contributed to any soaps. "People often ask me what I do with the male kids that are born," comments Christine, "and the answer is that we keep them and they earn their living as companions and celebrity soap stars. We would never put the male kids down."

Christine also makes a Christmas Croft Skin Cream, prompted by requests from customers for a sensitive moisturizer. "It got a lot of attention when a newspaper reported that a dairy farmer friend of mine was using it to very good effect on sore cows' udders." Good for cows, good for us! She is currently working on the further expansion of her range with Goosey Lucy's Egg Shampoo Bar; yes, you heard right. "It's made with egg yolk – although not always Lucy's as she's very good at hiding her eggs," she chuckles.

Christine's customers and the goats' fans can keep up to date with their antics on her website and even visit them at home should they venture so far north. "Some visitors turn up unexpectedly to meet the goats and see for themselves how the soap is produced," she says. "On one occasion I discovered a rogue photographer pinned up against the wall by the dogs!" The poor man got a cup of tea and a chocolate biscuit by way of apology.

Relying mostly on word-of-mouth to sell her products to customers as far-flung as Norway and the US, (courtesy of the internet) Christine caters to the increasing numbers of people who care about where their products come from. By cutting out the middle man, Gamrie Goat soaps are kept at a reasonable price whilst boasting an unquestionably traceable provenance. And anyway, isn't it time that our furry horned friends regained their rightful place in the pantheon of honoured fellow creatures.

the Gamrie Goat

THE GAMRIE GOAT

words } Amelia
photography } Amy Gwatkin
styling • Alex Cunningham
goat }{ Nat Miller
styling assistance ^ Chloe Bell

Little Shilpa

"Wear one and it changes your personality. Wear one and everybody turns." What could possibly hold this magical power? According to accessory designer Little Shilpa, it's a headpiece. More specifically, her own rainbow hued headpieces. For someone who's such a mad-hatter, it is somewhat surprising to learn that at one time Shilpa had never even heard of millinery. It wasn't until she was a fashion student in Mumbai that Shilpa discovered headpieces. Flicking through a hard-to-come-by copy of Vogue given to her by her flight attendant cousin she encountered the work of Phillip Treacy. "I saw his creations in there and I thought; can someone actually do this? And that's when I realised that there was something called millinery." Little did Shilpa know that within years she would so impress Treacy she would be offered an internship.

Shilpa's first professional foray into headwear began slightly bizarrely with the world of Miss India pageants. She made headpieces fit for beauty queens for three years before coming to London to hone her craft at Central Saint Martins. Following in the footsteps of her mentor Phillip Treacy, she would have loved the late Isabella Blow to have worn her creations. Perhaps Nicole Kidman would like to wear a piece instead? "There is a madness to her," laughs Shilpa, "but she is aware of her madness so it is very graceful!"

Little Shilpa doesn't only make an impact with her millinery, her jewellery designs also warrant lingering looks. When we meet she is wearing an eye catching oversized Bombay pin from her first accessories collection which, although large, seems humongous on her small frame. Yes, Little Shilpa is, as the name suggests, little. And I mean little, she's Polly Pocket proportioned! But what Shilpa may lack in inches she most definitely makes up in talent. Her designs often blur the line between fashion and art and last year she was invited to exhibit her found object fashion accessories at none other than the Victoria and Albert museum.

Waste not, want not – long an ethos for the thrifty and environmentally conscious amongst us – is a mantra that Shilpa keeps close to her heart. She refers to her work as 'rubbish', literally of course, due to its provenance. "I use really silly things," she says. Anything that turns up on the streets of Mumbai is considered fair game, from flip flops and bras to packaging and children's toys, all have found their way into her accessories. "I see something on the street, a shape happens in my head and I just have to make it!"

Shilpa creates strong pieces for strong "warrior" women. Paper cones become the vertebrate of a sea creature, and hulking acrylic medallions are arranged to look like armoured breast plates. "I saw a tarot card reader once," she explains, "and he said 'by the Chinese sun you are a tiger, which is why you're always looking for something powerful.'" Being a rather sceptical individual myself, I can't help but ask Shilpa if she's a 'believer'? "No... I don't know!" she says, before dissolving into mischievous laughter.

Shilpa describes her second retail jewellery collection, featuring paper umbrellas, feathers, chains, and plastic toy tanks, as "smaller versions of the larger conceptual pieces." She is worried that her toned down designs don't work as well as their larger cousins, but she must be doing something right because boutiques across the world are clamouring to stock her work. And with collaborative partnerships there is no need to tone anything down; "it's always, how mad can you go?!"

The madness of Shilpa's pieces is helped by a use of colour that mirrors an explosion in a paint shop. Shilpa assures me that this approach is a reaction to Mumbai which, much like London on the day we meet, is "very grey". Still, whilst the city may be grey the people of Mumbai are clad in full techni-colour. "If you look at Indians the one thing they aren't scared of is colour. They really use colour on themselves." Unconsciously proving her point, Shilpa is dressed in a vibrant turquoise get-up which quite literally puts my denim jacket in the shade.

Shilpa's crowning glories and jewellery pieces have gained fans both in India and the UK. I wonder if she can pinpoint the appeal her work has for both cultures? By way of explanation she says that "in India we have a really strong connection to Britain, which I didn't fully understand until I came to London and realised where the connection was coming from." In India she holds the unique position of being the only professional milliner in the country, which marks her out as "something new" and rather special, since "there aren't many people doing hand-crafted accessories."

As our drinks are now drained, I ask Shilpa what she will be doing in five years time. "I'll always be involved in handmade fashion and art, and as long as I get to change my medium all the time, I'll be happy." And for now? "I feel really lucky to be doing what I am – making incredible things out of waste. And the fact that I can also make some money out of it is amazing. I'm very thankful."

necklace worn as a head dress by Little Shilpa, blouse by Vanessa Bruno and dress by Modernist

necklaces by Little Shilpa, dress by Steve J and Yoni P, skirt by M-One

necklace by Little Shilpa, coat dress by Ashish and t-shirt stylist's own

words } Dearbhaile Kitt
photography * Yuki Kishino
styling   Kayoko Ishikawa
model }{ Dasha at Premier
hair   and make-up ° Teiji
using MAC and Shu Uemura
photography assistance
Maxwell Anderson

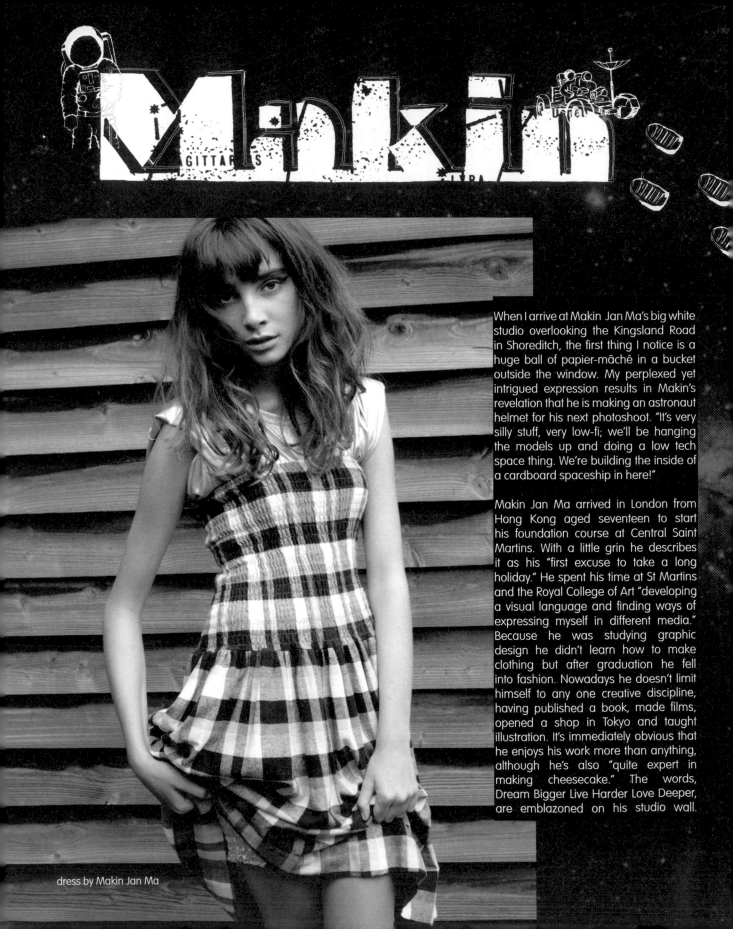

Makin

When I arrive at Makin Jan Ma's big white studio overlooking the Kingsland Road in Shoreditch, the first thing I notice is a huge ball of papier-mâché in a bucket outside the window. My perplexed yet intrigued expression results in Makin's revelation that he is making an astronaut helmet for his next photoshoot. "It's very silly stuff, very low-fi; we'll be hanging the models up and doing a low tech space thing. We're building the inside of a cardboard spaceship in here!"

Makin Jan Ma arrived in London from Hong Kong aged seventeen to start his foundation course at Central Saint Martins. With a little grin he describes it as his "first excuse to take a long holiday." He spent his time at St Martins and the Royal College of Art "developing a visual language and finding ways of expressing myself in different media." Because he was studying graphic design he didn't learn how to make clothing but after graduation he fell into fashion. Nowadays he doesn't limit himself to any one creative discipline, having published a book, made films, opened a shop in Tokyo and taught illustration. It's immediately obvious that he enjoys his work more than anything, although he's also "quite expert in making cheesecake." The words, Dream Bigger Live Harder Love Deeper, are emblazoned on his studio wall.

dress by Makin Jan Ma

words } Emma Hamshare

Not a bad message to wake up to every day! In this place creativity is life. Despite getting into fashion almost by accident, Makin is now making crazy constellation printed jumpsuits for Santogold and preparing to put on his first London Fashion Week show.

"I really don't know anything about fashion," he laughs. "I understand what I'm doing, but I can see there is still so much more to learn, and I like it like that." At the Royal College of Art, Makin was part of a collective called JanFamily. "We all had similar ways of thinking and working so we formed JanFamily to share ideas and make artwork together." They all lived together, intent on capturing the minutiae of their daily lives. "We made a book together as JanFamily called Plans For Other Days, and then we all moved on to different things in different places. Everyone is much clearer about their individual ideas, but the book and its concepts live on."

Small personal thoughts remain a vast source of inspiration for Makin. "Every season I do a chicken print," he reveals, unexpectedly. "My family owned a chicken farm, so I grew up with the chickens." He does this in memory of his beloved grandfather. "When I first started my label he was getting really ill, and just before he passed away I told him about my idea for a chicken print; so now I do it every season, to keep his memory alive." One jumper features the words I Love You embroidered hundreds of times over it in rows. It is part of a whole collection of work from his St Martins days, all about the intensity of obsession and how the more times those three little words are repeated the weaker the feeling behind them.

After he graduated Makin says, "I just let go of my thoughts and started making things." A Japanese buyer took some of his first clothes to Japan where they immediately sold. "So then I had to learn how to actually make clothes. I went out to visit factories but when I told them what I wanted they said, 'we can't help you unless you give us a production note!' So that's how I got straight into the real production side of things." As a result Makin won't design anything that is impossible to produce.

Makin makes observational short films that tell stories about his garments and even give them a personality of their own. The surreal Life Sucks But It Tastes Good features a boy with a bathtub on his back. Do the clothes or the film come first? "I write detailed scripts within which I describe what the characters are wearing, so then I end up making clothes for those characters," he explains. "The process of what comes first can get really messy in my head, but it's a game of constant translation; from writing to visuals to characters to clothes!" He always designs with himself in mind, but never concerns himself with what is currently happening in fashion.

The new You Are My Milky Way collection reveals Makin's sense of humour. It is inspired by "a love that becomes your entire universe" (hence the astronaut helmet). The imaginative catwalk show features a boy in a black and white cardboard space ship vrooming up and down the catwalk. "A lot of things that excite me most about designing a collection are not to do with the actual clothes," he laughs. "I try to design the collection quickly so that I can get on with the more exciting things!" I'm down with Makin. Cardboard spaceships – now what could be more exciting than that?

Sam wears trenchcoat, jumpsuit and hat by Makin Jan Ma, shoes by Baptise from Retro Man
Cat wears dress, jacket, head scarf and leggings by Makin Jan Ma, shoes by Retro Man, vest stylist's own

photography   David Poole
styling   Lucy Fine
models   Sam Rigby at Storm
and Cat at Models 1
make-up   Annabel Callum using MAC
hair ¶ and makeup   Eoin Whelan
using Illamasqua

Ladies and boys

These sentiments are immediately apparent when looking at Olanic's a/w 08 collection entitled The Boys, playfully inspired by the sartorial delights of school uniforms. Lashings of vertical white stripes on black adorn college knit scarves, Edwardian punk style blazers and beautifully cut high-waisted trousers. The collection is a mix of urban styling, lady-like grace and a dash of the unexpected (for example, tie-dyed denim resembling air brushed clouds). Niki says she can't escape the influence of street trends, but it is the element of elegance underpinning the collection that transforms the wearer into a head turner in the most subtle way. She is the girl whose quirky styling compels a double-take jerk of the head as you walk down the street.

Making the cut

Taylor realised that fashion was her true calling after three years spent studying art and design in Edinburgh. So she enrolled at the Scottish College of Textiles, where she developed a love of pattern cutting, lending a trademark sharpness to Olanic creations. On completion of these studies she began designing for the UK high street. With this experience behind her, Niki Taylor founded Olanic, an anagram of Nicola, in 2002. Olanic made its debut on the fashion stage at Paris Fashion Week in 2004. Since then the label has established itself on the London fashion scene; The Times tipped Olanic as 'one to watch' for London Fashion Week s/s 09.

London is not the only city

Although Niki shows at London Fashion Week, the Glasgow based designer feels no pressure to relocate to London. Not being based in the capital has helped to strengthen her Scottish roots, having recently worked with not one but two Scottish textiles companies; prestigious tartan manufacturers Lochcarron of Scotland, and Calzeat & Co, specialists in handcrafted fabrics. This has enabled her to create unique and exclusive fabrics which fit the theme of each season, making the process from drawing to garment a more fluid and complete one.

Collaborations are key

Niki loves to collaborate. "It's great to push myself and see my work used in a different medium." For the past six years she has collaborated with film maker and director Sandy Hutton to produce short films based around Olanic designs. The two have been friends for years and wanted to bring their shared sense of fun together in a creative outlet. "The great thing about collaborating is that you can fuse ideas and knowledge to create something entirely new, and it's a great learning experience for both sides." Niki's dream collaborator would be the acclaimed surreal film genius Michel Gondry.

Tokyo and Modernism

When not collaborating with others inspiration comes from cities; London, NYC, Antwerp, Paris, Portland, Oregon and Berlin are all places that get Niki's creative juices flowing. But for Olanic Tokyo provides the jack-pot for style inspiration. Modernism exerts a strong influence on Olanic's geometric cuts, and the fusion of art, music and fashion found in music videos offers up a host of less high-brow ideas, because, after all, it's just fashion.

Sindy dolls

Niki Taylor, aka Olanic, began making clothes for her Sindy doll when she was a mere nipper. Despite this precocious start, the adult Taylor tried her hand at graphics, interior design and fine art, before eventually trading her paint brush for a needle and thread and moving into fashion. Dropping the 36-18-33 vital statistics that Sindy is famed for, Taylor's mannequin became herself; "I design to suit me: styles with a sense of fun. I like to experiment with pattern cutting to create innovative shapes that are unique but wearable."

dress by Olanic, tights by Falke

words – Dearbhaile Kitt
photography – Jane Mcleish Kelsey
styling – Joan Campbell
model – Kinga Luk at IMG
hair and make up – Kim Brown at Premier using
Kerastase and Bobby Brown

Frankie wears top and trousers by Issey Miyake Pleats Please,
sleeve by Fred Butler

fred butler

Long before I meet her I have a very clear idea of what props stylist–cum–accessories designer Fred Butler will be like. I imagine a playful and imaginative character with a carefree, almost childlike approach to life; my preconceptions could not be more correct.

I meet Fred at her light and airy whitewashed studio in Angel, a space interrupted by small bursts of colour from her vibrant designs. Fred herself is equally as bright. Dressed from top to toe in canary yellow, she is the living, breathing epitome of her art. "I always wear one colour," she tells me, "I was blue yesterday and the day before I think I was white, it helps me to remember things because when I think of an event I think of the colour."

Fred is so soft–spoken that she is almost inaudible as she describes the night before, when she worked through the night until 6am to help her studio mate with an installation. Despite her quiet words she is full of energy – I only wish I looked as bright-eyed after a couple of hours of sleep.

Having worked on numerous prop styling projects for a multitude of magazines and stores over the past few years Fred has now officially launched her eponymous a/w accessories line. I ask how she first got into the world of accessories; "I studied fashion at Brighton University and during my sandwich year I went to New York where I worked for AsFour, who do styling, exhibitions, window displays and performance; so that opened up my eyes to a lot of different things."

Fred proudly shows me the look-book for her debut collection, Dodecahedron Collision, which features a bold assortment of multi-coloured asymmetrical forms, flung together like an explosion. I'm immediately intrigued by her possible inspirations. "All the ideas have been in hibernation since I completed my degree," she explains vaguely, "and I named the collection after an exciting 3D embroidery that I learnt to do just before I started." As I sit and listen I can almost imagine Fred during her younger days at school. It's quite likely she was one of those infuriatingly talented pupils whose natural creativity enabled her consistently to produce the best work in class – without even trying. "I think I just start making things really," she says, doing nothing to disprove my theory. "I never really think too much, so everything kind of comes out once I start working. I used a lot of triangles in the designs, but I think it was quite a subconscious thing."

Handily and somewhat thriftily, Fred sourced the materials for her collection from her leftover prop supplies. "There were so many materials that I didn't really know where to start. These," she picks up a prism shaped headpiece fashioned from a multitude of bright block colours, "were made from lighting gels left over from one job." I'm finding it hard to keep my eyes off her yellow painted nails. "I'm obsessed by bright colours so I like iridescent things that reflect the whole spectrum."

For Fred life is a constant process of seeking inspiration. "I don't like to waste my days off so when I get the time I enjoy going to see exhibitions," she tells me. "I also love going to bookshops; that's how I navigate around the city, I think 'ooh that's where that bookshop is.' I like looking for fashion photography second-hand books."

With work now going into her s/s collection, I wonder what the next step will be in Fred's career. "I'd love to make [catwalk] show pieces for young fashion designers like myself or I'd like to consult for a bigger brand," she reveals. The truth is that Fred's very success is based on her ability to ditch all sense of planning and allow instincts to run their course. If there is one thing that we can predict for this bold accessories designer it's that the future is set to be bright – literally!

Francesca wears jumpsuit by Aminaka Wilmont, top by Buddhist Punk, necklace by Fred Butler

words | Melinda Neunie
photography | Chiara Romagnoli at Wilde Hague
styling | Lilia Toncheva-O'Rourke
models | Francesca at Premier
Frankie and Jess Findlay-Brown at Models 1
hair | Sharon M using MAC
make-up | Nino Beckert at Soho Management

Jess wears top by Ashish, headband by Fred Butler

Krystof Strozyna

dress and bracelet by Krystof Strozyna, top by Eley Kishimoto, head piece made by stylist

words ｜ Emma Hamshare
photography ｜ David Fairweather
styling ｜ Oxana Korsun
model ｜ Rebecca Fleetwood at Models 1
hair ｜ Roy Hayward
make-up ｜ Philippe Miletto using Chanel

I meet Polish designer, Krystof Strozyna, at his New Generation stand during London Fashion Week. He is surrounded by his new s/s collection of fine hessian dresses with extremely long fringing, complemented by chunky coloured accessories and shoes with carved wooden heels. This collection is a significant change of direction for the man whose a/w collection is dominated by tightly constructed mini dresses in acidic brights and whites.

What inspired you to get into fashion?
Well, it wasn't so much an inspiration, more like a destination! Destiny! More like that. I never made any garments when I was little, but I did look at lots of British and American magazines. I could stare at one image for hours! I don't feel like I have chosen to do this at all. It chose me.

What are your influences?
Ah, well nobody in my family is even involved in fashion or art. So I don't come from a fashion background, and I don't think being Polish has influenced me directly. But maybe my new collection is a little bit folk... and many people work in the arts and crafts in Poland so I get things made over there.

How do you find living in England?
I came here four years ago to do an MA at Central Saint Martins. I was brought up in a very quiet little village so it was a major change to move to London. At first it was really exciting to travel into college on the tube, but it soon became hard work to drag things around on public transport. I learned a lot about fashion at college, but it was also really tough, learning about myself and how to live in a different country. I have learnt that I have to do everything myself because nobody is going to help me.

Do you think that designers are influenced by their surroundings?
Definitely, yeah! I love the mood of weird places like Arnold Circus in Shoreditch [in east London]. There is a small raised garden in the middle of all these old buildings [Victorian tenements] and someday I would love to live in a place like that, with the crows flying above. But at the moment I live in Battersea and there is no time for fun because I have too much work to do.

How do you design?
Well, the very first thing I do is a little research. I will have the whole idea in my head and then I start sketching little doodles before I draw in the details. After this I choose the things I like the most and try to work on them and develop them in the

right way. I want to make clothes for a modern woman who is strong but still feminine. I also like to experiment on a dummy. I work with simple silhouettes and try to make them interesting. I rely a lot on my intuition, but for things to work you have to be in the right place at the right time.

How is your new collection different from the first one?
It's more complex. Some of the knitwear looks sort of like an enamel, but it's quite soft. I've also used raffia mixed with silk and those pieces look nice from the inside too. I knew that I wanted to do something different. I had to get a good team together really quickly, so it certainly hasn't got any easier.

What do you think makes you unique?
I think the way that I work with jewellery in fabric is quite unique. The idea evolved when I tried to find something unexpected to put inside all these small pleat openings. I like working in ways that haven't been seen before and I hope that I can move the design of Krystof Strozyna forward with every new collection.

From the brightly hued power styling of his a/w 08 collection to the more subtle beige bucket sleeved creations that'll hit the shops next summer, it looks like Krystof Strozyna has got modern Polish arts and crafts fashion all sewn up.

dress, neck piece and cuff bracelet by Krystof Strozyna; top stylist's own tights by Wolford, socks by Uniqlo, shoes by Melissa at Sniff

^ black top, skirt and bracelets by Krystof Strozyna, stripey top and tights by H&M, socks by Franklin and Marshall, shoes by NDC
> dress, neck piece and bracelet by Krystof Strozyna, top stylist's own, tights by Wolford

^ dress by Krystof Strozyna, top, tights and socks by Uniqlo, shoes by Melissa at Sniff
< dress and bracelet by Krystof Strozyna, tops by Uniqlo, tights by H&M, shoes by Melissa for Vivienne Westwood at Sniff

Luxury jewellery and environmental responsibility rarely go hand in hand, but that is all set to change if Vivien Johnson of Fifi Bijoux has her way. I was lucky enough to talk to her about her label, the environment and how she is set on polishing up the future of the jewellery industry.

How did you get into jewellery design?

I studied Jewellery and Silversmithing at Glasgow School of Art, where I was quite experimental: my degree show was all crowns and tiaras! After working for museums and galleries for a few years I went on to work for a large jewellery company (that shall remain nameless) where I eventually became head of design. Over the years I became increasingly concerned about the negative implications of mining precious metals and gemstones because there is so little traceability. The whole production process was becoming of concern to me and once I became more informed I felt I had to seek change within the industry.

What prompted you to branch out and start your own company?

It's really hard to change things within a big company. For that reason I decided to start my own boutique label in the hopes of proving to the jewellery industry that there was an interest in ethically produced jewellery. It was a risk because I wasn't sure if there was the demand, but I figured the only way to find out was to pilot the idea myself. I really believe that there is an opportunity for our industry to do something quite magnificent.

How does the production process work for Fifi Bijoux?

We use gold panned from rivers by small-scale artisanal miners, who get a proper rate of exchange. Small scale mining is generally associated with extreme poverty so I often get to hear about mines from NGOs who are working in the field. For example I recently met a man from a Swiss NGO who works in Peru and has become involved in mining through his work with rehabilitating child sex workers who were trafficked there. Geologists who are conducting research in a mining area will also often become dedicated to improving the lives of the local communities.

What is your favourite gemstone?

Diamonds. I love them. I love unwrapping a new parcel and peering at their unique properties thorugh my eye glass. And I love seeing them in the jewellery. All the stones I use are special; the rutile quartz that I use to make my bigger showpieces is from Brasil where the profits are re-invested into community organic farming. The mine only has a few years left so all these pieces are limited edition, and once it closes the organic farm should take over as the main source of income for village. I've just come back from a trip out to Brasil and the miners taught me how to samba! But, on a more serious note, while we were there a local mine collapsed leaving thirty miners in critical condition. A few weeks before, a mine had collapsed killing over fifty miners – the mines don't even have basic safety equipment.

Do you feel that you are helping to change the industry yet?

I hope so. I talked to 200 delegates in Washington last year, including De Beers, Cartier and Rio Tinto (an enormous mining conglomerate). It's a bit like turning a ship on a penny, but there is a definite shift happening. It will take time, but I'm confident consumer demand will be the biggest driving force. I think that within five years we will see the adoption by the biggest industry players of a core set of achievable minimum standards.

Have you cared about environmental issues for a long time?

When I was young I was a member of the WWF and we went on lots of sponsored walks. I grew up in the countryside and that has made me very aware of any kind of negative impacts [from industry and so on]. I grew up close to the New Lanark cotton mills run by the reknowned philanthropist and educator Robert Owen, so I was always aware of how he managed to make a positive impact on the area.

What inspires your designs?

I tend to work organically. Pardon the pun! I travel quite a bit and I always carry a sketch book with me which over the months fills with lots of little notes and scribbles. There's never a dull moment. I then piece things together on a board and start to make stories out of them. I want my designs to have wide appeal so they are usually quite subtle and delicate. I couldn't imagine what I would do if I didn't design jewellery; it's what I've always done!

Do people ask you to make wedding rings?

Yeah, but as you can imagine men get really nervous. Sometimes I really have to trawl for as much information as possible. Wedding rings are part of such a huge emotional thing for men, but because they are so significant they tend to be really interested in the origins of stones and how a ring is made – it makes it a much more personal process.

FIFI BIJOUX

vest top by Sonia Rykiel, shorts by Rock and Republic, necklace by Fifi Bijoux

words } Tanya Geddes
photography * Jane Mcleish Kelsey
styling • Antonia Leslie
model)(Kasia at Next Models
hair ¶ and make-up ° Keneth Campbell
at Premier London

Vanessa da Silva

The professional life of Vanessa Da Silva is so multi-faceted it's practically kaleidoscopic. With so many collaborations, side projects and creative endeavors on her plate it's a wonder that she has the time to design her wonderful fashion range, let alone to meet with little old me to talk about it all.

I meet Vanessa in her remarkably serene studio-cum-living area, a space peppered with kitsch trinkets, perfumed with incense and coloured by the music that tinkles from her stereo. Vanessa is a psychedelic vision, dressed in a highly patterned and brightly coloured signature over-sized t-shirt jersey dress, her curly hair held atop her head with a long rainbow ribbon. The studio cat settles down next to us as we sit down to talk.

Vanessa hails from the Brasilian city of Sao Paulo, a place renowned for its hectic energy. "Brasil is a really culturally strong country – everything, the clothes, the music, the people, are just so... Brasilian," she says. However, after majoring in product design she decided to move to London in 2001. I wonder what on earth possessed her to relocate to our grey capital. "Even though Brasil is amazing I was getting quite bored in my work. Everyone's like 'oh my god, how could you be bored?!'" she laughs, "but I wanted a new challenge, I guess. So much is happening here and there is a sense that you can do anything, so I thought it would be exciting. And it is."

Vanessa's plans to undertake an MA changed quickly when she arrived, as she set about discovering what London has to offer; taking short course after short course in the city. After one particular stint at Central Saint Martins where she learnt experimental fashion design, Vanessa's path was set. She produced a few one-off garments for friends and installed a small range in west London boutique Euforia. Selfridges then got wind of the multi talented designer and decided to incorporate her work into their Brasil 40 Degrees promotion. They told her

that if she created a whole collection they would buy it, so being a 'try-anything' girl with a twinkle in her eye, she jumped at the opportunity. "It was quite a big order so it was really exciting! After that I got an agent and started getting orders from Japan, Hong Kong and New York. It was really cool but also slightly scary at the same time... but if you really want to do something you will find a way to do it!"

Vanessa has since worked on many diverse creative projects, including print designs for Brasilian fashion houses Reserva and Neon, prints for Basso & Brooke and accessories for Michiko Koshino. "I love collaborating with other brands," she tells me. Vanessa is also an accomplished illustrator, and her own clothing range is based on her drawn designs. "I think drawing is definitely my first love. I see clothes as a surface for me to put my drawings on, so I prefer to work with fluid shapes and I always work with jersey because it's more organic." Vanessa's illustrations have been instrumental in creating a vision for electronic folk band Tunng, with whom she has a long-standing relationship. "I would definitely love to do more stuff for bands," she enthuses. "I love music! Whenever I draw I'm listening to music, like pretty much twenty four hours a day. I'd like to be more involved in music; maybe I could do backdrops and stage sets... but I never seem to have enough time to do all the things I dream of."

Vanessa describes her collection as "kind of 70's... although not too hippyish. I only ever make the kind of stuff that I would wear myself and that usually means lots of loose styles and layering up. I love it when you can put a dress over trousers." It's this sense of love that oozes out of everything that Vanessa makes, from an album sleeve to a t-shirt dress, she has managed to bring a little bit of Brasilian magic to the drab streets of London town.

dress by Vanessa Da Silva, shoes model's own

words : Sarah Barnes
photography : Robin Jonsson
styling : Katie Burnett
model : Fanny at Next
hair and make-up : Joanna Lily using Makeup Forever
www.joannalily.com

dress by Vanessa Da Silva

necklace and shirt by Vanessa Da Silva

eggsellent

photography Amy Gwatkin
styling Alex Cunningham
assistance Chloe Bell

Aveda Dry Remedy Shampoo Aveda have been working in harmony with the environment for thirty years and now offer their beauty advice in shops across twenty four countries. They are also committed to supporting small craft-based communities like the Nepalese partners who produce the paper boxes for their gift sets. This dry remedy shampoo is perfect for hair in need of a big glass of moisture, featuring a blend of organic palmorosa, ylang ylang, rose geranium and a hint of vanilla; it promises instantly to transform straw-like hair into eminently flickable silky locks. **DK** www.aveda.com

Malin + Goetz Rice Bran Eye Moisturiser The stark design of Malin + Goetz packaging brings back to mind wild memories of primary school science, laboratory experiements and fooling around over hot bunsen burners. Created in a trendy New York neighbourhood, all products are based on 'hydration science' combined with a desire to maintain a natural pH balance. Fittingly, a clinical fusion of hyaluronic acid, rice bran and soya protein amino acids is found in this moisturising eye cream which works to promote capillary circulation, thereby reducing wrinkles and dark circles. **MN** www.malinandgoetz.com

Shea Alchemy Peppermint Foot Cream Don't make the cold weather an excuse to hide away and neglect your feet. North London founder, Sally, knows all about the demands of living in a fashion conscious city. Aware of its rough skin alleviating properties, she has stirred up a concoction of shea butter – sourced from a fairtrade co-operative in Ghana – and organic oils to create a delicious peppermint-scented foot cream. The sumptuous formula laughs in the face of winter and promises refreshing relief for cracked heels. **MN** www.sheaalchemy.co.uk

Pure Potions Skin Salvation Pure Potions was born from a mother's determination to create natural products fit for her daughter's dry skin. The result is a range of specially tailored skin rescue lotions for those who refuse to surrender to the bland industrial moisturisers available at the local chemist. The soft buttery ingredients have a soothing effect as they slide onto skin, leaving a sweet wine scent in their wake. **MN**
www.purepotions.co.uk

Caudalie Gentle Conditioning Shampoo Mathilde and Bertrand Thomas, the glossy couple behind Caudalie, are the perfect advert for great skin and hair care. Having met at university they have turned their shared love of cosmetics into a successful business. With all formulae based on the healing properties of grape skins, their conditioning shampoo is no exception. It boasts the delicate crushed petal aroma of the exotic sounding Fleur de Vigne, and will hopefully leave hair as soft and as shiny as that of the glamorous couple behind the brand. **MN** www.caudalie.com

Green People No Scent Shampoo Looking for a solution to her daughter's eczema, Charlotte Vøhtz founded Green People, ensuring all products are free from chemicals and artificial preservatives. Choosing to steer clear of evil petrochemicals and synthetic parabens, this unscented shampoo boasts natural foaming properties and is packed to the brim with aloe vera and olives to soothe even the most sensitive of skins. What's more, it's ultra concentrated, lasting three times as long as a normal bottle of shampoo. Perfect for these credit crunch times. **DK** www.greenpeople.co.uk

Neal's Yard Nourishing Lavender Shampoo Neal's Yard have for many years been the bastion of all things organically good. This nourishing shampoo comes in their trademark midnight blue bottle, reminiscent of an ages-old apothecary and including potion-worthy ingredients like sunflower and jojoba essential oils, but fortunately no eye of newt. The creamy texture is guaranteed to make the most unruliest of curls smooth and soft. **DK**
www.nealsyardremedies.com

Faith In Nature Crystal Body Deodorant Started in a small rural kitchen, Faith In Nature have devoted over thirty years to creating additive-free bodycare products. Their natural rock crystal roll-on is no exception. It works in perfect harmony with the body by tackling odour-causing bacteria so you're free to perspire without any of the unpleasant smelling affects. Hmm.. I wonder if it could possibly work on feet? **MN**
www.faithinnature.co.uk

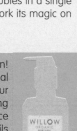

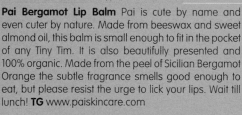

1. Caudalie Energizing Fluid • Pure Potions Skin Salvation 2. Faith In Nature Natural Crystal Deodorant • Pure Potions Camomile Baby Oil 3. Willow Organic Hand Cream • Trevarno Oatmeal Soap 4. Neal's Yard Lavender Shampoo • Lush Bath Bomb 5. Balm Balm Lip Balm • Caudalie Gentle Conditioning Shampoo 6. Pai Geranium & Thistle Combination Skin Cream • Lush Bath Bomb 7. Shea Alchemy Organic Lemon & Bergamot Hand Cream • Juicy Lucy Muscle Rub Lush Bath Bomb 8. Malin + Goetz Eye Cream • Soapnut from Akamuti 9. Shea Alchemy Peppermint Foot Cream • Lush Bath Bomb 10. Malin + Goetz Eye Cream • Willow Organic Face & Body Wash 11. Shea Alchemy Organic Lemon & Bergamot Hand Cream • Trevarno Oatmeal Soap 12. Neal's Yard Lavender Conditioner • Lush Soap 13. Aveda Caribbean Therapy Body Cleanser • Hubble Bubble Organics Organic Green Clay Face Mask 14. Pai Geranium & Thistle Combination Skin Cream • Pai Bergamot Lip Balm 15. Willow Organic Hand Cream • Cinnamon Stick from Willow Gift Box 16. Trevarno Organic Day Cream • Trevarno Soap 17. Hubble Bubble Organics Organic Rosemary & Orange Bath Salts & Scrub 18. Aveda Caribbean Therapy Body Cleanser • Faith In Nature Chocolate Shampoo 19. Aveda Dry Remedy Moisturizing Shampoo 20. Pure Potions Skin Salvation

Lush Bath Ballistics With a brand now recognisable in thirty countries worldwide we can trust Lush to know a little thing or two about the slippery business of bath unguents. Available in a variety of soft pastel shades and fruity aromas, each bath ballistic releases a delicate perfume when dropped into warm water, ridding the mind and body of any troubles in a single puff. Now if only I could get one to work its magic on ex partners! **MN** www.lush.co.uk

Balm Balm Lip Balm Having bagged the Best Organic Beauty Product award in 2007, Balm Balm is proving to be more than just a catchy name. Unlike so many overpoweringly scented lip balms, this natural and mild rose geranium number is so gentle you can even apply it on other areas. So for those cold wintry months where crackly skin breaks out, apply this balm to ensure more than just glossily smoochable lips. **TG** www.balmbalm.com

Willow Face And Body Wash For Men Attention men! This one is for you. Only certified organic jojoba essential oil makes it into Willow's gel wash, to ensure your conscience stays as clean as you do. The skin saving properties of aloe vera will cleanse not only your face but your body and the spicy citrus and cedarwood oils will leave you with a manly scent. All Willow's products are beautifully packaged (in biodegradable materials), meaning that they would make the perfect gift for that someone special. **DK** www.willowbeautyproducts.co.uk

Trevarno Rosewater And Camomile Skin Toner Celebrating their tenth anniversary this year, Trevarno is inspired by the beautiful Cornish estate where all their products are handmade. Containing rose and camomile flower water mixed with gentle antibacterial camomile properties, benzoin, lavender essential oils and grapefruit seed extract, this makes for one refreshing mix. Use it after cleansing come morning or night for a truly refreshing glow. **TG** www.trevarnoskincare.co.uk

Pai Bergamot Lip Balm Pai is cute by name and even cuter by nature. Made from beeswax and sweet almond oil, this balm is small enough to fit in the pocket of any Tiny Tim. It is also beautifully presented and 100% organic. Made from the peel of Sicilian Bergamot Orange the subtle fragrance smells good enough to eat, but please resist the urge to lick your lips. Wait till lunch! **TG** www.paiskincare.com

Juicy Lucy Natural Deodorant Made from an appealing concoction of eighty four skin-loving minerals, including yummy sounding organic floral waters, essential oils, cypress water and (maybe not so yummy sounding) odour neutralising Himalayan rock salts, this natural deodorant conditions skin at the same time. Feeling your best the natural way has never smelt so sweet. **TG** www.juicy-lucy.net

Hubble Bubble Green Clay Face Mask Don't be turned off by the name's likeness to toads, wizards and sorcerers. While the slushy seaweed-green mixture may slightly resemble the contents of a witch's cauldron, the effects are somewhat less menacing. Hubble Bubble products are made with natural ingredients designed to improve emotional wellbeing, and this 'raise positivity and reduce stress' philosophy has been successfully squeezed into a gentle hydrating mask, which leaves skin tingling with freshness. No witchcraft included! **MN** www.hubblebubbleorganics.co.uk

Neal's Yard Remedies To Roll Energy Many of the products offered within the Neal's Yard treasure trove are fit for the pages of a fairytale. With a cold and flu remedy just right for Sneezy alongside stress busting tonics ideal for Grumpy, the company have now created the perfect potion to combat our Sleepy tendencies. The sweet herbal scented oils in this energy stick promise an instant mind and body boost with a single stroke over pulse points. A fabulously discreet way to survive the work-day after a boozy night. **MN** www.nealsyardremedies.com

skirt and top by Carin Wester, hat and shoes by Paul Smith, tights model's own

words } Catherine McColl
photography * Aya Sekine
styling • Britta Burger
models ⨡ Tijana and Callum Wilson at Select
hair ¶ and make-up ° Maki Tanaka
styling assistance ^ Hannah Jones

Carin Wester

Not since Vikings ruled the sea has Britain seen such a wave of Scandinavians storm our shores. No need to secure the battlements just yet, this era's invasion comes in the guise of super-hot designers rather than aggressive men in longboats. At the forefront is Carin Wester, a designer keen to play clothing Cupid and mad for a bit of old skool Salt-N-Pepa

Of course, as a child Carin was, like any self-respecting designer-to-be, obsessed with dressing up in clothes from her mother's huge wardrobe; but it's refreshing to learn that she wasn't obsessed with studiously learning all the big names in Vogue. Oh no, it's much better than that: "When I was nine I heard Madonna's first album at a school party and after that I spent several years trying to become her. I even took a lot of dancing courses," she says. Before I get a chance to ask whether her quest to become Madonna involved conical bras, I'm overwhelmed by her next revelation: "Then everything changed when I started junior high; Madonna was out and I started to dress up like Salt-N-Pepa. I wore a lot of baggy trousers, shiny bomber jackets and crazy accessories with that look." Carin, it seems, is not one of those precocious designers who strives to maintain a mask of impenetrable coolness.

After a moments silence to honour the era that was Salt-N-Pepa, I ask Carin for her opinion on the influx of Scandinavian designers into the UK fashion scene, a movement which is helping to define a new aesthetic: "I think Scandinavian designers have become very popular of late because we make very wearable yet still fashionable clothes in a very strong way. And I think that all of us work at a very good price level, so that people who are financially limited but love good design can afford to buy our clothes."

Carin loves to play with strength and vulnerability in her designs; "masculine tailoring in womenswear was something I felt was missing in Swedish fashion, so when I began designing it became an integral part of my look," she says of her design philosophy. "I really like it when a women looks perfect in something that she's borrowed from her boyfriend. And in my menswear collection I have tried to break away from that very skinny, leather masculine rock 'n' roll look to create a much more feminine silhouette with softer comfortable cuts. Essentially I want to create the perfect outfit for a boy to wear when he goes to see his girlfriend's parents for the first time!" Boys of Britain take note: the trend for wearing clothes that make you look like an emaciated heroin addict is O-V-E-R (except you, Russell Brand).

Carin's inspiration reveals a plethora of literary and film references, including the works of luminaries such as Gertrude Stein and ficticious characters like Huckleberry Finn. Somewhat bizarrely, for s/s 09 Carin has imagined what would happen if the Dutch character played by Sylvia Kristel in the 1974 movie Emmanuelle, and the gardener from Grey Gardens – a 1975 documentary film set in New York – met each other. "Since I make both menswear and womenswear I always base my collection on some kind of love meeting between two figures. First I go through the collection trying to visualise the feeling of it, then I start to play with the theme more to show it very clearly within the fashion show. Everything is based on that story: from music to invitations to make-up and hair. The moment you enter my fashion show you should feel all the ideas come together."

Carin is unashamedly honest about the financial pressures of trying to run a fashion business and admits that "it's very good press to have someone famous in my designs. As soon as a celebrity wears something people start calling like crazy wanting to buy the same outfit." She's keen to become a commercial success since "this is something I should be able to pay my bills with, not just something that's a lot of fun!" Unafraid to be who she is, say what she thinks and design what she likes, Carin Wester answers to no one, and with such prodigious talent she doesn't need to. (Plus, who would cross someone with Viking blood in them?)

coat, trousers and long sleeve t-shirt by Carin Wester

howies

David and Clare Hieatt, co-founders of howies, have been idols of mine ever since I discovered the label through their lovingly designed catalogues: the new winter booklet has just flopped through my door as I write this, and contains the usual inspiring mix of digestible yet thought-provoking articles on catching your own fish for supper, how to make an oak table without glue and why we should return to the art of real bread-making, alongside aspirational (in the best possible way) photos of normal looking guys and gals hanging out in the stunning Welsh countryside not far from where the howies head office is based in Cardigan Bay. Product shots are broken up with snappy poems, and snazzy illustrations from the likes of Supermundane, bold imagery which also makes its way onto the t-shirts which are printed in short runs at their on-site warehouse. howies specialise in ethically produced performance clothing and have achieved a huge fanbase for their range of sturdy denims and high quality New Zealand merino wool garments, a collection that includes snug hoodies, cute patterned blouses, stylish jeans and striped undergarments. High fashion it isn't, but wearable and long lasting? Hell yeah.

Determined to meet David and Clare in their home environment, I set about wangling tickets to attend the inaugural Do Lectures, a four day event intended to inform and inspire people to get off their backsides and, well, do something. I arrive at the Fforest campsite in drizzling rain to discover that I will be sharing a large designer teepee with an assortment of other girl attendees, including my friend and fellow climate activist Tamsin Omond who has been asked to speak about her actions. Complete with deerskins to sleep on, wood burner and a large decking area, it feels like real luxury. That is until, in typically Welsh style, it proceeds to pour for the entire duration of our stay and we discover that even swanky luxury tents can leak.

To attend the Do Lectures anyone could handwrite an application and post it to the howies team. Emails were not accepted, which led to such memorable efforts as a home baked cake and an etched piece of wood. There was apparently a surprising amount of disbelief in the necessity for this time-consuming process called letter writing from a generation more used to the

click of a mouse. Seventy five lucky people were then offered a free place, made possible because howies have in place an Earth Tax, whereby 1% of sales or 10% of pre-tax profits are spent on grassroots and environmental projects.

David and Clare are keeping a low profile during the lectures – preferring instead to allow the younger members of their team to coordinate the event – so it is some time before I am able to pin down the two founders. Eventually we take a seat at one of the long tables in the communal dining area, hastily erected on the windswept hillside to accommodate nearly a hundred hungry campers. Dressed casually in their best howies gear they are quietly spoken to the point of reticence, but brighten up considerably when we start discussing the ethos behind their brand.

The couple come from the same small town in Wales, and were hanging out as friends from their schooldays. "She dumped me a few times when we were young," chuckles David. By their early twenties they were living together in London where they had taken up jobs in advertising. "David and I talked about leaving London from the moment we got there," admits Clare. "We always knew we wanted to be somewhere remote." Having found their ideals somewhat tarnished by the glossy world of consumerism the Hieatts – still working fulltime – set up howies in 1995, producing t-shirts in their flat. David admits that he never really set out to make clothing, seeing it more as a means for effecting change in the world. "I always dreamed I could start a company full of bright people with great ideas that would make others think." The Do Lectures is therefore the natural culmination of all this work. "This is the dream bit [taking shape]!" he says. "I'm not that into fashion, but I am obsessed by quality and good design and I thought I could use the production of clothing to do important things, like this."

howies has grown slowly and steadily, eliciting many a faithful fan along the way. "It took six years to draw our first paycheck," says David. Then seven years ago they took the plunge, ditching the security of their jobs and moving back to Wales in pursuit of their dream. "It was a way of doing what we love in a place we love whilst bringing up the kids," says Clare. The couple now have two opinionated young girls who are consulted over important business decisions such as the controversial plan to sell part of the company to behemoth Timberland a few years ago. "We had a serious meeting with the kids about going into business with Timberland," says David. "And that really simplified things for us. Their main concern was 'are you going to be home for bathtime?'" So that clinched the choice. Some of their customers were more than a little bemused by the decision to sell part of the business, but the couple felt they had no other option, having already remortgaged their house twice to keep the company going. David comments that it is a constant struggle to grow the company whilst still retaining its personality. "I feel we can effect more good in the world if we are bigger. It is a kind of justification for growth," explains David, "but it's not perfect. [The performance wear clothing company] Patagonia have been a real inspiration to us as to how we can do that. But because we make things we are part of the problem. I just hope that we can utilise making stuff as a tool for change." It's been a few years since the buyout though, and the cracks are starting to show. "Timberland don't interfere in any of the creative stuff but in my heart I do feel a loss of ownership," says David.

The awe-inspiring partnership between David and Clare is at the core of howie's success. "Doing it together has kept us going," says David. "That and a combination of naivety and stupidity, especially when what we are doing doesn't make either sense or money." They remain full of new ideas. "But are they

businesses or hobbies?" asks Clare. "We've got a farm now and we're growing our own vegetables. It's a hobby but it could become more because we're both very interested in food." "I'm more 'let's do it' and Clare's like 'let's not'," chuckles David. "I'm the voice of reason," she counters. "David started howies, and I helped out for a bit, thought it was quite interesting and now I've taken over." "We drive each other nuts but we've never had any major differences over the business because we know each other's reactions so well." says David. Is it possible to keep work away from family life? "We are good at being away from work, especially at the weekends, but we do inevitably talk about work at dinner or when people are staying with us," reasons Clare.

Clare is much more interested in the design of the clothes, following the production of garments from start to finish. "Designing each range is a long slow process because we have to make sure that the clothes are fit for purpose; that you can do things in them and keep warm and dry, but still look good in the pub." The mountain bikers and skateboarders amongst the howies staff often contribute their expertise, and if a range does particularly well or badly they have no worry about changing direction. Many designs are unisex and the new brochure features a Girlfriend sweater, inspired by the vast quantities of men buying last season's womenswear design Humbug to wear themselves.

Clare and David are utterly committed to instigating social change, and have created a web-based lending library – just choose one from a range of inspiring books and post it back when you're finished. They are acutely aware that humans cannot carry on as we are, so they have high hopes of putting together another Do Lectures next year: change cannot come fast enough. "We reassure ourselves that humans are the smartest creatures on the planet, but it took 2,000 years to put wheels on luggage!" comments David. He worries that these Do Lectures will not reach enough people, so has made it a priority to record everything so that the lectures are easily accessible on the accompanying website. "With our Big Little Voice lectures last year we were teaching skills to make a difference. This time it's all about inspiration. We thought, who would we invite to a dinner party?" The chosen speakers include author and campaigner Alistair McIntosh, organic farmer extraordinaire Guy Watson, cradle-to-cradle designer Michael Braungart, cult thinker Tim Ferris and the Surfers Against Sewage activist Andy Cummins.

Throughout the Do Lectures we are fed amazing home-cooked food by delightful local ladies. Evenings are spent singing songs around a fire, taking an illicit sauna, setting the world to rights in the cosy bar area or listening to a band in the giant teepee where the lectures are held, nestled into a dent in the sharp cliff remains of an old slate quarry. By the end everyone is buzzing with ideas and energy, friendships have been forged and plans are afoot to set the world to rights. There are many types of Doers in this world, but the unassumingly tenacious Hieatts are amongst the most inspiring of all; now all that is needed is for us to go forth and spread their ideas as far and as fast as possible. One day all businesses will care this much.

www.dolectures.co.uk

Jordan wears t-shirt and skirt by howies, necklace made by stylist

Jordan wears top by JW Anderson and trousers by howies, Anton wears trousers by howies, vest his own

words Amelia
photography Robin Jonsson
styling Katie Burnett
models Jordan and Johan G
at Modellink and Anton Ford
make-up Tara Mears using MAC
photography assistance Victor Halling

GOSSYPIUM

AND

Amelia's magazine

Many children of the 70's will remember with fondness their mothers running up an exciting new garment on the family sewing machine. Clothkits was the iconic Lewes-based brand that revolutionised the concept of making your own clothes, providing in kit form all you needed to make up a whole outfit. From the specially printed fabric; ready to be cut, assembled and sewn, to the buttons and thread in just the right shade to finish it off, everything was included in a neat little package that arrived in the post. And with canny concern for any unnecessary wastage the small areas of spare fabric between the main design were often printed up with smaller matching pieces – for young girls this often meant a matching fabric doll and for their mothers it invariably meant a cute co-ordinating shoulder bag.

Clothkits catalogues featured members of this very family-orientated business, and had all the charm of an album of snapshots. Scrolling through the years we can watch the various personalities growing up, wondering at the identities behind the natural smiles and carefree posing. Clothkits was most notable for their bold use of print design, which made their clothing instantly recognisable. Often a pattern would be printed in only one shade onto a bold selection of berry and woodland colourways, which were then teamed with thick tights in fabulously bright hues. Natural fabrics like babycord and thick cotton twills were favoured, with matching sets of skirts and waistcoats or dresses and jumpers all the rage. Popular patterns were repeated year after year instead of conforming to the latest trends.

But alas, as the 70's crept into the 80's the rampant consumerism that came to characterise the decade soon made the idea of making your own clothes a dated concept. Clothkits adapted by focusing more on their popular striped jersey separates but, much to the dismay of their loyal customers, eventually the company disbanded altogether. Now, with a surging interest in crafts amongst many young fashion-savvy people, the time is ripe for a renaissance in kit fashion. After years of buying cheap and shoddily made identikit clothing from the high street many cool young cats are once again ready to make their own unique garments, safe in the knowledge that the only person who will have laboured over the item will be the one wearing it. This time around, though, kit fashion has an ethical conscience that can be traced right back to the farms where the cotton is grown.

Gossypium shares more than a passing identity with the original Clothkits brand, for it is also a small family company – owned by wife and husband team Abigail and Thomas Petit – based in the eccentrically artistic town of Lewes high on the picturesque Sussex Downs. Specialising in the production of 100% organic and Fairtrade-certified soft as clouds cotton apparel, Gossypium has collaborated with Amelia's Magazine to produce the bag kit that comes free with (most copies of) issue 10.

Textile engineer Abigail used to work as a consultant for Agrocel, which seeks to ensure that small scale farmers in India are able to run viable sustainable businesses on the global market; encouraging organic practices and bio-diversity whilst guaranteeing the purchase of crops. While based in India for a couple of years she was able to learn first hand right from the bottom of the supply chain just how much of an effect Fairtrade practices can have on a farmer's life. She experienced the dreadful inequalities inherent in the trade when she was welcomed with open arms into the textile mills who had refused entry to the farmers, and was luckily able to astound the owners with the fantastic quality and whiteness of the products from organic farms. "I will never forget the expression on one mill manager's face when he saw the first bobbins on his desk," she says. Abigail believes that much of what she did in India was cultural, "really understanding how the world looks from the viewpoint of a cotton farmer, and teaching them a bit about how we westerners think." Trying to break down two hundred years of post-Industrial Revolution segregation was no easy feat, "and it took a lot of patience, openmindedness, risk and passion – on both sides."

Gossypium now works in partnership with Agrocel (who also supplies much of the high street with Fairtrade cotton), but this is not the only coupling that was forged during those heady years spent in India. Abigail met Thomas on the job and it seemed only natural to set up both a business and a family together on their return. "I remember being really amazed that I had met someone who seemed to understand everything that I was trying to do," she comments. "No one I had ever met before saw textiles in such a timeless and quality driven way. We were just friends at first, but we got so joined together by this project that we married in 2004 and added a couple of kids to our joint responsibilities!"

The couple still visit India every year in order to foster stronger relationships with their partners and supply factories, who are chosen for their ability to grow, weave and print organic fabrics within a localised community. "We know each other so well now that when we speak on the phone it is as if we are just down the road from each other," she says. "It's a very special way of doing business." Gossypium's core business is the production of staple cotton garments such as men's shirting, babygrows, yoga-wear, bed-linen and underwear which favours perennial style over monthly trends, but to these base lines have been added a few kit fashion packs. These inspired Amelia to approach Abigail with the aim of working together on designs for a matching dress and bag that would emulate the high quality Clothkits clothing she wore as a child. Working in tandem with talented textile designer Brie Harrison they have come up with adventurous and colourful designs for kit fashion that is not only highly desirable but also eminently ethical.

words } Dearbhaile Kitt
photography * Chiara Romagnoli
styling • Oxana Korsun
model }{ Anna Thompstone at Select
hair ¶ Naoki Komiya
using Bumble & Bumble
make-up ° Molly Outken-Davies
using MAC and Nars
assistance ^ Bianca Korsten

dress and bag by Brie Harrison for Amelia's Magazine at Gossypium, poloneck stylist's own, frilly shirt by Tibi, hat from Beyond Retro, bracelet by Leju, socks by Fogal **To order this limited edition dress at a 15% discount visit www.gossypium.co.uk and enter the discount code AMELIA**

HOW TO MAKE YOUR BAG KIT

1 Cut along the red lines, but leave the 2.5cm margin at the top of each bag piece as you will need this for hemming.

2 Fold the margin over along the red line and sew along.

3 Place the hemmed bag pieces with the patterned side facing inwards. Leaving a 1cm seam allowance sew around the three sides of the bag leaving the hemmed section open. Turn back the right way.

For the straps there is the option of having one long across the body strap (follow step 4) or two shoulder straps (jump to step 5).

4 Place the bag straps with the pattern sides facing inwards. Sew along the width to join the two pieces as close to the edge as possible, to give you one long strip.

5 Fold your strap(s) in half lengthwise. Press to shape with edges inside, pin down and top stitch.

6 Sew your strap(s) onto your bag.... Ta-daaaa! Your kit is now a bag!

words } Dearbhaile Kitt

art profiles

The Girls

words } Tanya Geddes

Andrea Blood and Zoe Sinclair are The Girls, a pair of, erm, girls, who have made art together since they first met at school in Dorset. Following a stint on the art foundation course in Bournemouth they both secured places at Central Saint Martins and moved to London together to share a flat in Brixton. Here they began to collaborate on a series of self-portraits that toyed with notions of what it means to be English, going on to garner multiple prizes including the prestigious Observer Hodge Award. Claustrophia set in not long after and The Girls went their separate ways for seven years before reuniting in 2006. Now in their early thirties they are still buzzing with the excitement of working together again. "The time is now. We don't take anything for granted," they tell me. Having finally bagged their first solo show at the Beverly Knowles Fine Art Gallery this autumn, they are jittery with the possibilities of what is to come.

The Girls are surprisingly sedate and look like twins; both wear black and sport short blonde hair with pale white skin, the only obvious physical difference being the black-rimmed rectangular glasses that Zoe is wearing. Apparently their twin-like demeanour extends to a paranormal fluency, for they constantly finish each other's sentences and admit that they often know what the other is about to say before she utters a word.

From tongue-in-cheek self portraits painted on a pair of breasts to a spooky portrait of Myra Hindley, their work is quirkily provocative. What inspires their creations? Zoe confesses that she is an inveterate hoarder of charity shop ephemera – with a specific fetish for old magazines and postcards from the 1920's. "We both collect things obsessively and occasionally we take mini holidays together for the sake of research, which is always fun. We like visiting dirty bars!" jokes Andrea. She attributes their preoccupation with nostalgia to early childhood experiences. "We both had loads of story books but limited toys compared to what kids have nowadays, so we made our own toys and dolls' houses out of cardboard. Our toys were always a bit... different," she says gleefully. Andrea is better at paying attention to detail. "Working together as two people means that we are able to be much more dynamic, creative and opinionated," confirms Andrea.

I wonder what their first impressions of each other were. "I thought Zoe was dark and subversive," laughs Andrea. For her part Zoe perceived Andrea as "beautiful, mysterious... much quieter. I discovered her darker side when we embarked on our foundation course; one of her projects focused on suicide and I liked the way that it was naive, yet dark at the same time." Finding in each other a kindred spirit it was a natural progression to work together, and they were soon creating a series of saucily erotic self portraits. "We enjoy getting into character and putting on a costume, and it's easier to control the environment if you use yourself as the model."

Nowadays they come up with ideas separately and share them by email. "I collect reference materials and scrapbook with them, then I sketch more ideas and email Zoe," says Andrea. Zoe also religiously jots down ideas in her notepad, often the result of "alcohol-fuelled brainstorming."

They are both extremely, almost see-through, English-rose pale. "Someone once said to us 'be careful girls, you're not just white but very white,'" explains Zoe, "and yes we do speak well and to an extent you can't escape what you are." So instead of denying their intrinsically English heritage, they play to this very quality. In the series Friday Mermaid a mermaid eats fish and chips in the bath and dries her seaweed out on a collapsible washing rail in what looks like a tenement backyard. In E102 a girl lies collapsed in a woodland, surrounded by the debris of what might be eaten at a typical English children's tea party. Perhaps all those E numbers got too much or perhaps she ate a bit of Fly Agaric by mistake: a couple of plastic rabbits gaze on helplessly.

In their colourful performance piece Garden Party – which I am lucky enough to view in person at the preview of their solo show – The Girls explore our relationships to food, power and desire. Drawing on the Japanese idea of Nyotaimori, which is the daring practice of eating sushi from the body of a nubile young lady, The Girls subvert the idea of a traditional English tea party. In the accompanying stills, what looks suspiciously like a vicar picks uncomfortably at cucumber slices, swiss roll rounds and strawberry tarts, all arranged artfully on the pale and prostrate body of one of The Girls.

Most recently they have paid homage to the Smurfs, who turned fifty in October of this year. For their Smurfette series one of The Girls dons an over-the-top blonde wig, merkin and fake breasts before daubing herself from head to foot with blue body paint and posing unashamedly in traditional British settings; next to a sandcastle bearing Union Jacks on a beach, or on a heather moorland surrounded by cards evocative of the Alice in Wonderland stories. The Smurfs have become something more complex – jokey seaside femme fatales mutate into a commentary on our relationship to childhood, sexuality and what it means to be English.

Clearly The Girls do not take themselves too seriously so I think it apt to ask them how they would sell their work in a lonely hearts advert. "Attention seeking 1950's starlet seeks adoration by millions... and book deal," is the reply. Enjoying this silliness, we talk about what animal each would be and why. Andrea decides that she would definitely be "an albino killer whale" which makes Zoe laugh. After much prompting she plumps for the slightly less concise "albino animal in an albino zoo."

From the green hills of the Dorset countryside to the hubbub of the London art world, these most English of girls are determined to shake up our concepts of who we are in some of the most charmingly underhand ways possible.

Jon Elliott

words } Amelia

Eerily-lit stacks of crumpled televisions, bloated belly-up computer monitors dribbling electronic guts and noxious rainstorms of shattered components. These are the matter of Jon Elliott's enormous and daunting collages of disastrous apocalyptic landscapes. The reality of the toxic nightmares that we are creating every time we send old electrical equipment to landfill are rendered tangible, causing the viewer to pause and review the incredible waste our society has permitted us to create. Indifference is no longer a possibility – the physical nature of our trash is writ large in front of our eyes.

Jon studied biological science for two years, but turned towards art as he became increasingly intrigued by the rise of technology and its attendant effects on our consumerist culture. He is not an activist but rather a commentator, one of a growing body of artists who hope to persuade "people to look at themselves and their cultures through a new lens." Principally employing paint as a medium because of its apparent indifference and detachment from the subject matter Jon Elliott also picks up old parts with which he can collage and create three dimensional installations.

His current obsession with technology dates back to 2004, when he created a series based on abstract patterns, for the exhibition Glitch. His intention was to reduce basic biology to a complex pattern of bits, not unlike that of computer data, which would take on a life of its own. "The process of painting elaborate patterns was tedious, so I would invariably mess up individual shapes, and since one shape led to the next the overall pattern would change and grow more complex, hence the title of the exhibition," he explains. "Bits of those patterns are still included in my paintings even now." A growing frustration with rampant consumerism was by now becoming too much for Elliott to ignore and he became obsessed with trying to reveal the truth behind what he saw all around him. His paintings mutated into technological wastelands with a strong ecological message.

For Nightmare On Grand Street, Elliott during the course of three months in 2005, collected twenty-eight computers and TVs off the streets of his hometown of Brooklyn; he then stripped the contents of this electronic scrap and invited other artists to paint and etch on the screens, which were then lit with lanterns. "One old TV that I found was stuffed full of dead cockroaches, and because I hate the idea of finding live bugs inside one I haven't brought home any more abandoned goods since then," he says. "In the future I'll use what I already have in storage, or I'll bring screwdrivers out with me to open them out on the street first." He has been known to recycle his own obsolete equipment for use in sculptures and has managed to salvage enough technology from the streets to build his own computer.

Jon makes pieces titled with threatening names such as Plague Of Excess, Tidal Debris, and Fortress, for he believes that we are now bombarded with potentially brainwashing ideologies on a day to day basis, both consciously and subconsciously. "Advertising and consumerism are inescapable, and with the boom in technology that has occurred since the 1980's the internet has become the dominant force in disseminating

information; able to inform aspirations and desires, and even shift our belief systems."

He believes that the internet is a major perpetrator of an obscure "technological mythology" of which he has "many fuzzy impressions but few concrete notions." Jon, a keen reader of science fiction – "good science fiction is simply philosophy in a narrative form" – is well aware of the impact of popular media. Whilst he has no interest in the banal or kitsch aesthetics of popular culture, he acknowledges that everything from commercials and electronic music to UFO cults and Scientology are "visions of the power of technology interacting with consumer culture." These new mythologies have the potential to fullfill deep psychological needs that are not otherwise being met, but are also capable of abstracting reality in many other inherently destructive ways. In short, Jon is sceptical of these technological mythologies, and his current collection is a response to this fear.

Jon's sinister piles and slumps of trashed and obsolete screens – menacing conduits of consumerism – flicker with oddly familiar images of consumer culture that hint at Jon's disgust with the current state of humanity. These dark musings are often embellished with the subtle wonder of decorative pattern, a beauty at odds with the carefully incorporated

subliminal messages; for Jon would prefer his viewers to form their own opinions. "I want to confront the agents of our modern mythologies with everything they have left out, and are continuing to leave out."

Ironically, the internet has been of fundamental importance in Jon's research process. Over the last four years much of his inspiration has been found by searching for information with keywords such as 'wasteland'. His Nightmare On Grand Street project draws strongly on reports discovered online that detail the export of toxic electrical scrap from the USA and other technological nations to countries such as China and Africa. Up to 18,000 shipping containers of toxic waste have been deposited abroad under false pretences – with hopes of recycling projects leading to nothing more than a cheap buck for the exporters involved.

Modestly, Jon concludes with the hope that whatever he is learning through the act of creation can be conveyed to others. He is one of many forward thinkers who are proving that green is no longer just a colour; it's an inescapable way of thinking to which we all must turn.

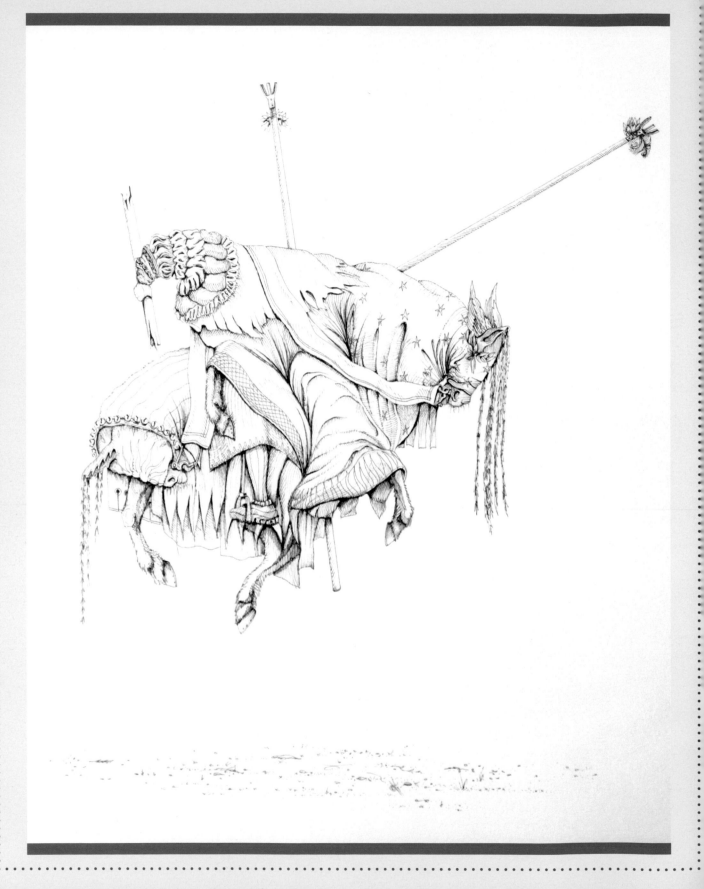

In the depths of south London lies a big white house with a big white fireplace in a very white room full of well-to-do looking people chatting animatedly amongst themselves. They are here to see the work of Michael Whittle, whose precise black ink drawings on clean white paper line the walls of the Man & Eve gallery. Exacting yet warped, Michael fuses the intricacies of the medieval mind with fantasies all his own. In Knight, floating horses are intricately conjoined with randomly protruding human arms and lances, piled atop one another in a jousting contest gone horribly wrong. In Barber a curious creature – is it human? – pokes his finger in a large circle into a seated figure's head. The extruded finger is covered in tiny seedlings. Escher-esque, a contorted rocky mass hovers in Aerial, possibly named for the bent tree fork hanging out into the great white ether. Following Marcel Duchamp's famous mandate 'The title of a painting is another colour on the artist's palette' names hint at multiple interpretations and text is hidden in piles of rocks and stones. Landscape With Deep Symmetry parts I and II show a cross section of a human brain, lovingly mapped and numbered, as if for some professor of biology.

It therefore comes as little surprise to learn that mop-haired Michael was once a student of biomedicine. We are in a room upstairs in the immaculate gallery-house, where I must strain to hear the quiet exclamations of this mild mannered man. "I

not be in their normal frame of mind.

On graduation he was offered a place to study sculpture at the prestigious Royal College of Art, which was an eye-opening experience. "You could hardly walk ten paces without having to stop for a really interesting indepth conversation, which could be really annoying when all you wanted was a cup of tea," he laughs. "Everything I thought I knew about art was turned on its head, so that by the time I finished I was full of questions." On leaving he discovered the joys of the Rotring pen. "It's very hard to practice sculpture without a large studio – it's so much easier to just sit at a large table and draw. In fact it was entirely my sister's boyfriend's fault that I started drawing again when he gave me this bloody pen!" He now lives in Kyoto, Japan with his wife, whom he met thanks to another stroke of luck. "She was at the RCA too but we didn't meet until I won the scholarship [in Japan] that she landed the year previously. We fell in love in a sushi restaurant. Crazy, isn't it? It was the start of a long distance relationship. I could have been a walking advert for Skype – sometimes we wouldn't even talk, we'd just leave our computers on in our studios so that we could hear each other moving around, even coughing. Sansung would play me music from the other side of the world."

Michael is engrossed in how knowledge is produced, labelled and maintained, how human beings attempt to tame

Michael Whittle

words | Emma Hamshare

had to choose between art and science," he says, "so I chose science, but my dad gave me drawing lessons once a week." Towards the end of his degree in Bradford he had an epiphany whilst visiting some modern art museums in Germany, where his old desire to create came flooding back. "It was all very romantic," he smiles. "I came home and pushed all the furniture to one side of the room and made drawings all over the walls... I fell back in love with art." He decided to take a year out to pursue his dreams. "But I never went back [to science]. It's great!" he chuckles.

During a second degree in fine art at the Duncan of Jordanstone College of Art, Michael won the first of many scholarships, to study at Konstfach Art College in Sweden. Unfortunately it was winter and he found that the constant twilight has unexpected consequences. "They get very existential and dark in the winter; it's like being in an Ingmar Bergman film! I would be walking down the street and these huge lights would shine out of the church windows, glowing like nuclear devices," he says. Even more strangely there were special notices stuck up all around the college to inform the international students that because of Seasonal Affective Disorder many people would

nature, construct and decipher sensory worlds. I mention the drawings left behind by vetinary students I once lived with, how complex and beautiful the diagrams and names of muscles were. "Biological words have such a beautiful history behind them," he agrees. "They are part of a framework of ideas that represent an obsessive interest in why we are here." So his intricate slices of brain are rendered as networks of signs and pathways to ideas and thoughts, a desertified landscape furrowed with dead-end canyons. "The underlying structures of my drawings are taken from the first comprehensive anatomical studies of the brain made in the 19th century," he explains. "It's really amazing – the early scientists would describe parts of the brain in the same way you would describe a landscape, with valleys and hills used to describe all the little lumps and bumps in there." Areas are populated with tiny herbs, roots and berries, for Michael has a healthy wonder for the knowledge of the ancient medicinal healers, who intuitively knew what mushrooms were good and which were deadly. "And I like the idea of a mandrake plant – you pull it up and underneath there's a little man screaming! Fascinating!"

In many of his drawings the people have really long fingers. Michael chuckles, "I started to collect early medieval prints, and everyone seemed to be pointing in them. Next time you're in a museum you should check it out. Some of the reasons are quite obvious, like the man pointing to his wife's belly as if there's a child to come." In other pictures there is no apparent reason for the pointy finger. "In one, a man is pointing at a skull popping out of the pocket of someone's jacket... it's a very strange technique." Michael decided to reappropriate the idea in his own work, but with hyper-extended pointiness. "They add a really strange interpretation to everything else that is going on," he explains. In Chronica Nobilissimorum a man's pointed finger punctures the pregnant belly of the woman standing next to him and curls all the way over them both, dripping root-like appendages. "My wife brought me up on that one actually," admits Michael. "She wonders how becoming a father might affect my work... and I'd love to see how becoming a mother affects hers!"

Living in Japan is creatively invigorating but means that Michael must consider the symbolism of his work even more carefully. "Things can have a completely different meaning there," he says, furrowing his brow. "Often I will find myself looking for something universal that can be understood across the world." Never have the endless creative possibilities of the human mind been more evident. As I carry my overloaded but inspired mind home it is full to the brim with fantastical floating landscapes, pokey little robed men and squealing mandrakes. From the tiniest marvels of nature to the greatest details of our world, Michael maps it all so wonderfully well.

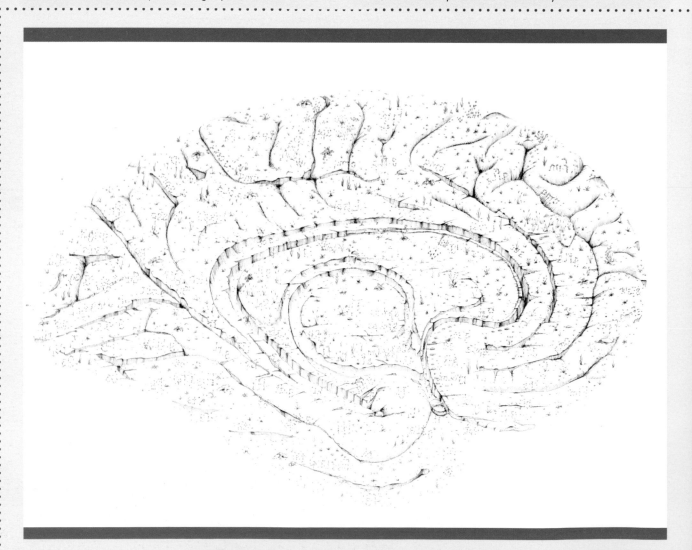

David Cotterrell

As I walk down the unusually quiet thoroughfare of Brick Lane I idly follow the moves of a sandy-haired man in front of me. Strolling alongside his bike, he has the easy air of a travelling man and I find myself wondering if he is David Cotterrell. A few minutes later I can't help but smile; sometimes your initial instincts really are correct.

We step inside the coffee shop and settle into the comfy sofas, surrounded by pockets of murmured conversations. Despite David's laidback demeanour, it soon emerges that he is busily engaged on several projects. After all, he is an installation artist whose work encompasses video, audio, interactive media, artificial intelligence, device control and hybrid technology. "Because I'm interested in so many different issues I can go off on tangents, but the same narratives re-emerge all the time."

We at Amelia's Magazine discovered David's work earlier this year at the Tatton Park Biennial, held in Cheshire. Here he erected a series of pieces inspired by the Red Book for Tatton Park, a book about creating grand gardens written by the famous eighteenth century landscape gardener Humphry Repton, in which he advised landowners to "test people's spatial

words } Tanya Geddes, photography * Joel Prince

perspectives of the grounds" through judicious management of nature and artifice. Whilst cribbing up for his commission David was mightily impressed by the story of the family behind Tatton Park, and especially with the insatiable collecting of the family's last heir, a man named Maurice Egerton. Despite the absence of a successor, he was devoted to the upkeep of his family gardens and continued to travel the world, making additions to the ancestral collection. But of course his continued dedication failed to cheat death, and the estate is now in the hands of a trust.

So bemused was David by the presumptious notions laid out in Humphry's handbook that he set about offering a modern day interpretation of his ideals, manipulating reality through careful design. To do this he created a number of perspex artworks featuring idealised views, and these modern day frescos were hung throughout the gardens for unsuspecting visitors to chance upon, in the hope of prompting them to question the authenticity and meaning behind a typically picturesque scene.

David is also inspired by larger themes such as war: to this end he was invited to Afghanistan late last year, spending one month with medics and later on, one month with the civilians of Kabul. "The Wellcome Trust scouted me to contribute to a major exhibition based on their work of the past few hundred years. They gave me training in first aid so I could hang around doctors who work in the field and see how they cope with their work, but fortunately I didn't have to use it," he explains. "At first they were nervous [of my presence] but eventually I became invisible. When I returned later, I found myself – through force of habit – carrying combat application tourniquets, first-aid field dressings and mine clearance equipment in my camera bag." He forged many unexpected friendships during the trip, not least with a character known only as Major. "It was a revelation to me [to find

out] that despite their (literally) uniform appearance, the military is comprised of very diverse people." When he decided to return to Afghanistan in April it was to get a more realistic sense of the people and place. "I kept a hundred page diary," he exclaims. "I don't usually write, but I scrawled nonstop. It is likely that my brief visits to Afghanistan will have a lasting influence on my future work." He is currently producing a "panoramic installation" that will feature video and photography for the Wellcome Galleries exhibition later this year.

David is "intrigued by stories, experiences and attitudes that are hidden" especially when juxtaposed against traditional renditions of history. "At school I was forced to read the radical historian Christopher Hill, and he introduced me to an amazing idea," he says. "History is never a simple sequence of great events, but rather an infinite number of smaller narratives. From these, depending on your viewpoint, you can always find something that makes sense, however illogical it may seem." Fragmented experiences and altered perceptions of environment remain the central intrigues in David's work. "I grew up in east London in the 80's, where housing estates sprung up in the blink of an eye." Within a few years each owner was desperately trying to make a unique mark on their home; in the process they often replicated each other's attempts. "More than one house was surrounded by gnomes. There is something so heroic about people's wish to modify their landscape."

Bearing all of this in mind, David is wary of the narrow perspective the art gallery-going elite affords his work. "I believe that there is more to art than merely producing luxury goods for wealthy customers." His worries are especially poignant given that a desire to unearth bypassed stories is one of his key ideologies. Luckily projects like the one at Tatton Park make his work available to a far wider viewing public.

Sarah Baker

It's a classic tale: life imitates art. Sarah Baker found herself living inside the pages of a Jackie Collins novel. Keen to interview the Queen of Trash, Baker – a strong and determined lady – had been emailing Jackie's celebrity photographer son-in-law to help set up a meeting. Emails flew back and forth between the artist and celebrity photographer, but then – nothing. The celebrity photographer had gone mute. Thoughts flashed through the artist's mind over possible reasons for the breakdown in communication; was she supposed to sleep with the celebrity photographer to meet with the queen of trash novels? Or was his (Hollywood) wife an insanely jealous creature who couldn't stand her husband liaising with a pretty young artist?

Three years passed and Sarah was by now consumed with her current project Studs, which takes a sideways look at Jackie Collins' infamous novel The Stud. Filming in America, Sarah discovered the novelist would be in Arizona as she was passing through. This time determined to meet with Jackie, she marched into the casino on an Indian reservation, with a portfolio of work under her arm. Needing no introduction or indeed the help of a celebrity photographer, she easily persuaded Jackie Collins to do the interview she had longed for. Smart, strong women always get what they want.

In Sarah's own words, art was forced upon her from a young age. Her parents inhabited the art world and her parents' friends were all artists, who in turn encouraged her to become an artist. She even went to a Fame-type arts high school (leg-warmers were optional). But Sarah resisted all the encouragement and Fame schooling, wanting instead just to travel. It was when Sarah was cycling across the USA with a "crazy couple" she had met at a bar one night, that she decided that in the end art did make sense for her.

Hackney, where we meet at Sarah's studio, cuts a sharp contrast to the celebrity world she often parodies. The American born artist has lived in London ever since doing her MA at Goldsmiths, University of London and she seems to have picked up a few English habits; she offers me tea and biscuits when I arrive. Watching Sarah, stonewashed denim clad and bespectacled, dunk biscuits and slurp tea, I can't help but think once more of the contrast between this Sarah Baker and the seven foot high cardboard cut-out glammed-up version of Sarah Baker propped against the studio wall.

With the recent proliferation of celebrity weeklies the interest in celebrities has reached an unprecedented level, but the escapism provided by the ups and downs of someone else's life has existed since the 1960's, when bands like The Beatles and The Rolling Stones were transformed into the modern day constructed celebrity that Sarah finds so interesting. It was Jackie Collins who began to document this life with the release of seminal trash novel The Stud. "The Stud is really contemporary, despite having been written in 1969," says Sarah. "The main character is very materialistic; always talking about Gucci and Louis Vuitton. She is a strong powerful women who uses her sexuality to gain power and money, and this was a fairly new concept in the 60's and 70's. Nowadays we are still really intrigued by this lifestyle, so the book still seems very realistic and relevant."

Studs stars Sarah Baker, Bill May and Wes Studi. Bill May is a synchronized swimmer. Chuckle you may; for this is exactly the reaction that Bill has had to overcome to become the best in the world. It is this that Sarah, a former synchronized swimmer herself, finds so intriguing, having also previously worked with him on the video piece A Portrait Of Bill May. Likewise Wes Studi, the Native American actor, has had to overcome social stereotyping to work in the Hollywood film industry. Bill and Wes' involvement brings the idea of defined cultural representations to the forefront of discussion, mirroring Jackie's themes in The Stud.

Playing The Bitch is Sarah, The Rich Husband is played by Bill May and Wes Studi takes on the namesake of the book; The Stud. Studs focuses on the inter-relationships of the characters, highlighting their obsession with power and money. Sarah is intrigued with the ability of high status brands to denote

status to their customers, and in a nod to the out of control consumerism of Jackie's novel the monographs used by classic fashion houses are overlaid on top of one of Bill May's swimming scenes. Because she is interested in deconstructed narratives the continuity is continuously severed, and some stills from the film have been collaged over in post-production; Wes is shown adorned with Jackie Collins' hands, a reference to the costumes that he has previously worn in Dances With Wolves and The Last Of The Mohicans. Playing cards are superimposed over a scene in reference to the fact that Jackie Collins stays at the gambler's favourite Venetian Las Vegas Hotel when in town. Ironically, Sarah was dealt four aces whilst playing poker in Las Vegas, thereby enabling her to finish financing the project.

Sarah had originally planned to interview Jackie Collins purely for research purposes, but soon decided to include parts of the interview, in which Jackie "adjusted herself and did whatever it was that made her look as if she had had a face-lift" in Studs. As a medium, film is equally freeing and challenging for Sarah. "For Jackie Collins to appear in the piece may not have been the original plan, but guess what? Artists can do what they want! With painting there are edges and boundaries. But when an artist makes video it's not a commercial, it's not a music video, it's not selling anything, it doesn't need a narrative and it is a completely open, time-based medium. Then again, what is the purpose of it? How do you know when to stop?" As a viewer, Sarah admits, she can be very critical. "Video can be really awful when it's rubbish.

I walk away [if something is bad] and I think you should too. No one should have to sit through something boring or pretentious." Sarah was still grappling with the length of her Studs video montage when I spoke to her, but assured me that it would be under ten minutes. In part, so people don't take her own advice and walk out during screenings! To challenge the viewer's preconceptions of artists' films she will make an "open ended collage, so that the viewer is left asking a question."

Sarah believes that emotions are also more easily evoked through film. "I sang Whitney Houston's I Have Nothing for one of my videos, and because I can't sing it made everyone laugh instead of inspiring feelings of yearning!" She was pleased with this response and has decided that maybe it's the combination of sound and visuals that is so potent in film. "I guess a painting can [evoke strong emotions], but it's more common in film. Maybe it's the way we look at things, or the familiarity of viewing. We are far more used to viewing TV and Hollywood films than art, and a close second to TV is looking at images in magazines."

Perhaps this explains why Sarah gets so much of her inspiration from flicking through magazines. "Art inspires me, but it doesn't get my juices going as much as a good fashion spread." She is particularly intrigued by fashion advertising. Fittingly, Sarah has collaborated with cult magazine Vague Paper. "Magazines are a really powerful venue for my work as many more people get to see my pieces," she admits. "They are the perfect place for my art to be seen, on someone's kitchen table with a coffee stain on it."

Crafty Scarves

concept and photography * Jessica Dance
set design ^ Robert Müller and Jessica Dance
model X Robert Müller

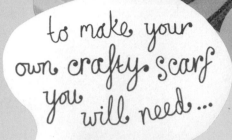

to make your own crafty scarf you will need...

An old pair of jeans,
A needle and some
embroidery thread,
An un-picker,
A pair of scissors,
A pen.

1

Being careful to save the button,
cut your old jeans in half by
chopping up through
the crotch.

youch!

2

Remove the pocket from the bum of
your jean leg by using an un-picker
to undo the stitching. Then, sew the
pocket back on in an upside-down
position.

3

Draw a foxy outline, like the one
below, onto the jean leg and then
cut out the shape.
You will only need
to cut through
one side of
the jeans.

a curved belly will
fit better round your neck

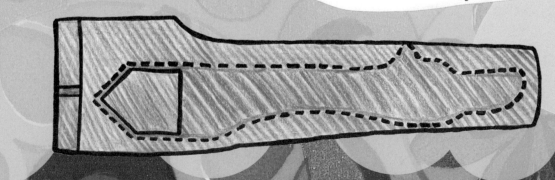

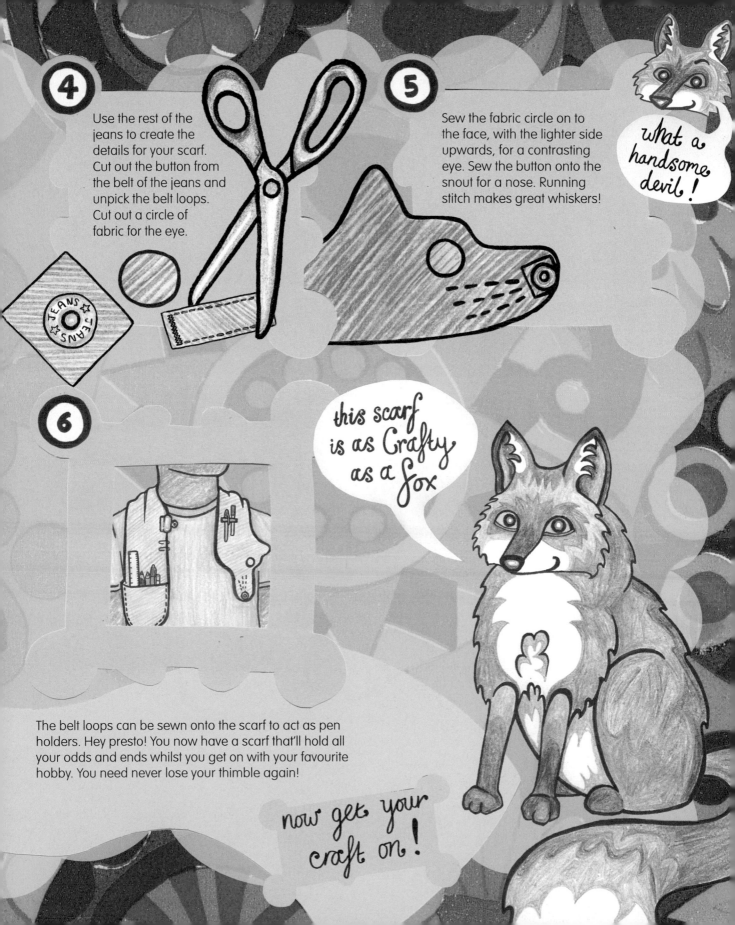

4

Use the rest of the jeans to create the details for your scarf. Cut out the button from the belt of the jeans and unpick the belt loops. Cut out a circle of fabric for the eye.

5

Sew the fabric circle on to the face, with the lighter side upwards, for a contrasting eye. Sew the button onto the snout for a nose. Running stitch makes great whiskers!

what a handsome devil!

6

this scarf is as crafty as a fox

The belt loops can be sewn onto the scarf to act as pen holders. Hey presto! You now have a scarf that'll hold all your odds and ends whilst you get on with your favourite hobby. You need never lose your thimble again!

now get your craft on!

You **SPIN ME** RIGHT **ROUND**

Tom wears sweater by Paul Smith, trousers by Thomas Burberry, boots and bag model's own, bike supplied by Bobbin Bicycles

photography • Gemma Booth at Santucci & Co
styling • Oxana Korsun
make-up • Peita Gregory at Balcony Jump using Stila
models • Octavia and Frankie at Models One, Sam at Storm,
Sylvia, Anna T, Marianne, Robyn H and Brooke at Select, Tom
from Bobbin Bicycles, Stefan Zander, Chris, Evgeniy and Pouwa,
Gus, Sebastien and Mike at Fixed Gear London
photography assistance • Alex Forsey, thanks • Laurent

Frankie wears top by Paul Smith, cardigan by Eley Kishimoto, shorts by Peoples Market, shoes by Melissa for Alexandre Herchcovitch at Sniff, sunglasses by Retrosuperfuture at Number 22, tights by Uniqlo, Abici Svelina bike supplied by Velorution

Evgeniy wears shirt by Comme des Garçons for H&M, trousers by Thomas Burberry, shoes by NDC, mac by Erotokritos, belt by Lacoste, bag by Paul Smith.
Marianne wears jumpsuit by Emilio de la Morena, cape by Cacharel, shoes by H&M, hood by Rag & Bone, socks by Paul Smith.

Robyn wears T-shirt from Andy Warhol collection by Pepe Jeans, jacket by Levis, waistcoat by Kenzo, Delile by Antonio Marras, shorts by Sass & Bide, tights by Wolford, shoes by Marc by Marc Jacobs, thanks to Clara and Lulu the dog.

Brooke wears striped sweater by Eley Kishimoto, pink sweater by McQ Alexander McQueen, trousers and shoes by Lacoste, socks by Paul Smith, bag in the basket by Comme des Garçons for H&M, hat stylist's own, Brompton P3L bike supplied by Velorution.

i love

all animal.

photography * Amy Gwatkin

pictures

The Upsetters

photography * Gerald Jenkins
styling • Harris Elliott
models)(Josephine at Storm,
Sycha Mubiaya and Robert Gatonye at D1
hair ¶ and make-up ° Gary Gill for Monroe using MAC
Pro and Wella Pro, www.garygill.com
styling assistance ^ Camilla Denno and Teddy Poku

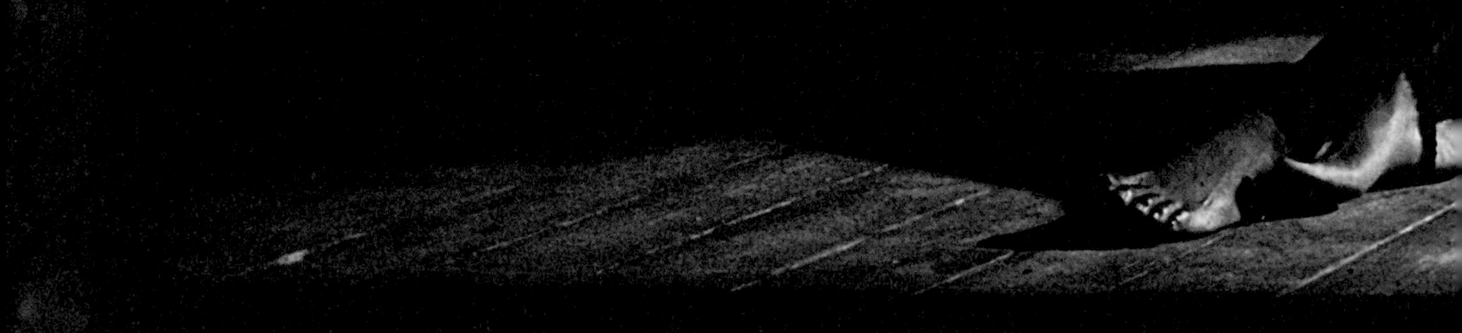

Sycha wears vest by Preen, tights by Emma Cook, bracelet from Pebble

Sycha wears neckpiece by Rowan Mersh, vest by Preen, tights by Emma Cook, bracelet from Pebble, hat from Beyond Retro

Robert wears shirt by Carhartt, trousers, hat, braces and belt from Beyond Retro, shoes by Timberland Boot Company, bowtie by Paul Smith

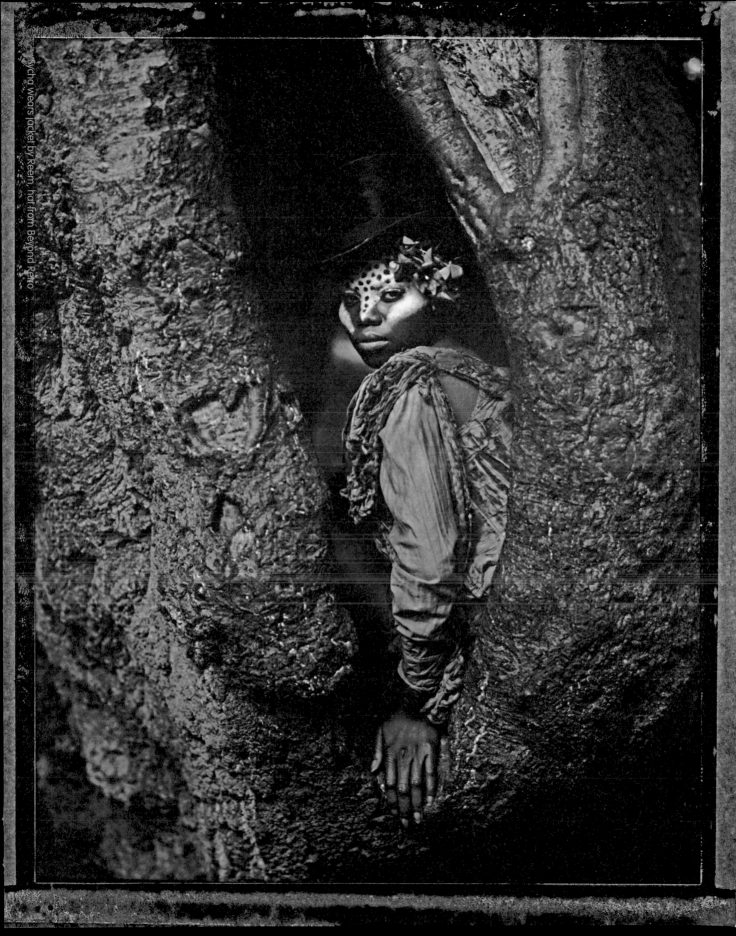

Sycha wears belt worn as headpiece by Bryce D'Anice Aime

IN COLOUR WE AMBLE

Tamara wears trousers by M by Missoni, poloneck vintage from Oxfam Boutique, vest by People Tree, gloves by Paul Smith, boots by DKNY and hat stylist's own (vintage Kangol) Anna wears trousers vintage Sportsmax, poloneck by Uniqlo, scarf by Sonia Rykiel, gloves, hat and socks by Paul Smith and sandals vintage Marc Jacobs

photography   Chiara Romagnoli
styling   Oxana Korsun
models   Anna Thompstone at Select and Tamara at Profile
hair   Naoki Komiya using Bumble & Bumble
make-up   Molly Outken-Davies using MAC and Nars
assistance   Bianca Korsten

Anna wears stripey top vintage Marc by Marc Jacobs, dress and bag by Brie Harrison for Amelia's Magazine
at Gossypium, gloves by Sonja Rykiel, hat by ParkVogel, tights by Fogal, socks by Paul Smith

Tamara wears stripey top by ParkVogel, waistcoat by Paul Smith, skirt by DKNY, bag and hat vintage Clothkits, belt from Beyond Retro, tights by Fogal

Tamara wears top by Sonia by Sonia Rykiel, shirt and vest by Cacharel, scarf by Malene Birger, hat from Beyond Retro, gloves by Paul Smith, tights by Fogal

Anna wears top, hat and trousers by Cacharel, poloneck from Oxfam Boutique, cardigan and socks by Paul Smith, necklace by Leju, sandals by Vivia. Tamara wears poloneck by Uniqlo, stripey top by Paul Smith, hat and dress vintage Clothkits, scarf from Beyond Retro, socks by People Tree, sandals vintage Michael Kors

photography • Natalia Skobeeva

MONUMENTAL MOAI

KINGSnorth

words } Amelia
photography • Julia Kennedy
styling • Susie Lloyd
illustration ~ Laura Quick
models)(Rupert at FM, Christopher at Fugere
Silvia and Kate Ellery at Select
hair ¶ Ben Jones using Bumble & Bumble
make-up ° Jo Frost using MAC Pro
photography assistance ^ Iain Graham and Meg Mackay
styling assistance ^ Liz Mansfield
make-up assistance ^ Thomas De Kluyver
thanks to Stoke Boat Club

Kingsnorth is the battle ground for our future. This rickety old coal-fired power station on the Hoo Peninsula in Kent is nearing the end of its life, but the government and energy giant E.ON would like to build the first of seven new coal power stations across the UK on the same spot.

Will this lead to the apocalypse? Well, if the UK starts building new coal fired power stations again it is not inconceivable that the future will look like this. Coal is by far the most polluting form of energy there is, so building new plants will send a clear message to the rest of the world that we are not serious about investing in the green technology and energy efficiency necessary for tackling Climate Change. Not only will we fail to meet our own emissions targets as already set by the government but we will be encouraging the growth of the coal industry globally, leading inexorably to runaway Climate Change.

Once we pass the tipping point of Climate Change global temperatures are predicted to rise by up to 6°c in the next one hundred years. This means that by the end of this century many people will be displaced from their homelands as glaciers disappear, deserts spread, severe weather intensifies and sea levels rise by up to five metres. Populations on the move will fight over increasingly scarce food, land and resources.

Sound apocalyptic yet? Maybe Climate Change doesn't exist. Maybe it's just a crazy idea dreamt up by scientists. But what if they're right? Wouldn't it be better to try and prevent this great experiment with our planet, just in case? To do that we need to act now. Every individual has a voice, and together we are strong: we can put a stop to the building of new coal-fired power stations like the one at Kingsnorth.

www.climatesafety.org
www.climaterush.co.uk
www.climatecamp.org.uk
www.wakeupfreakout.org

The End Is Nigh

Rupert wears coat by Soar, shirt by Nudie, waistcoat/scarf by Siv Støldal, kilt by Noki, belt by Kenzo, jeans and boots model's own
Silvia wears snood by Kenzo, jumper, leggings and boots by Stella McCartney. Kate wears jacket and trousers by Ashish and shoes by YMC

Christopher wears jacket and scarf by Barbour, helmet by Little Shilpa, boots by YMC, sweatshirt and jeans model's own, Silvia wears jacket by Eley Kishimoto, dress by Meadham Kirchhoff, boots model's own, Kate wears bodystocking and tights by Galjon, blanket by Vivienne Westwood, socks by Barbour, boots by YMC, Rupert wears jacket by Hardy Amies, jumper and trousers by Peter Jensen, boots model's own

Christopher wears jacket by Barbour, sleeveless jumper by Old Town, bobble hat by Ashish, -shirt and jeans model's own, Silvia wears dress and shoulder accessory by Louise Gray, arm warmers by Lou D

Rupert wears jacket and trousers by Lou D, necklaces by Pebble, Eley Kishimoto and Tom Binns, shoes by B Store and jumper as belt by Barbour

Kate wears jumper by Alban, skirt by Vivienne Westwood, tights by Galion, shoes by YMC, painted necklaces by Pebble, shell necklaces stylist's own. Rupert wears poncho by Rag & Bone, headdress by Pebble, top stylist's own

Kate wears jumper by Alban, skirt by Vivienne Westwood, tights by Gallon, shoes by YMC, painted necklaces by Pebble, shell necklaces stylist's own. Silvia wears dress and shoulder accessory by Louise Gray, arm warmers by Lou D, boots model's own. Rupert wears poncho by Rag & Bone, top stylist's own, headdress by Pebble, trousers by YMC and boots model's own. Christopher wears his own clothes and a vintage cape.

Kate wears coat and skirt by YSL, leggings by Kenzo, leg warmers by Cooperative Designs, scarf by Hardy Ames and boots by YMC

Rupert wears jacket by Hans Madsen, jumper by McQ Alexander McQueen, scarf by Barbour

The End

Rupert wears cardigan by McQ Alexander McQueen, waistcoat by Paul Smith, shirt by Rag & Bone, trousers by Old Town, Christopher wears blanket by Vivienne Westwood, Silvia wears jumper by Cooperative Designs, leggings by Kenzo, boots model's own, Kate wears cape and dress by Vivienne Westwood, leggings by Rag & Bone, boots by YMC, mittens by Cooperative Designs

THE TRAP

REBEL, BUT THERE IS NO ESCAPE.

photography * Chiara Romagnoli
styling • Emma Macfarlane
model ⅃ Suki at IMG World
hair ¶ Mark Daniel Bailey at Artlist Paris using Bumble & Bumble
make-up ▽ Annabel Callum at Naked Artists using MAC Pro
photography assistance ^ Amy Gwatkin
styling assistance ^ Jessica Charlesworth

top and skirt by Ann... and knickers by Agent Provocateur, bracelet by Maison Martin Margiela, boots by Sonia Rykiel

jacket by Rick Owens, bracelet by Maison Martin Margiela, trousers by Christopher Kane

leggings by Vivienne Westwood, belt by Anna Vince, bustier by Alessandro Dell'Acqua, bracelet by Maison Martin Margiela

jacket by Rick Owens, body suit by Bjork McElligott, bracelet by Maison Martin Margiela, skirt by Veronique Leroy

top by Rick Owens, nipple covers by Agent Provocateur

bustier by Viktor & Rolf, glove by Paule Ka, skirt by Yohji Yamamoto, tights by Bernard Willhelm, bracelet by Maison Martin Margiela, boots by Sonia Rykiel

everything is connected

Everything that ever was, is and will be was born from a star, to which it will inevitably return. In the meantime humans have cunningly evolved ways of changing matter into stuff; digging materials out of the ground, making things, and then throwing them away without really considering any of the implications for our little planet Earth. Where once we were aware of our great interconnectivity with the cosmos we have created a huge disconnect, rarely noticing along the way that the things we treasure most are not things, but the relationships we have with one another and our world.

Sofia Andersson

Kate Slater

Cat Laulgan

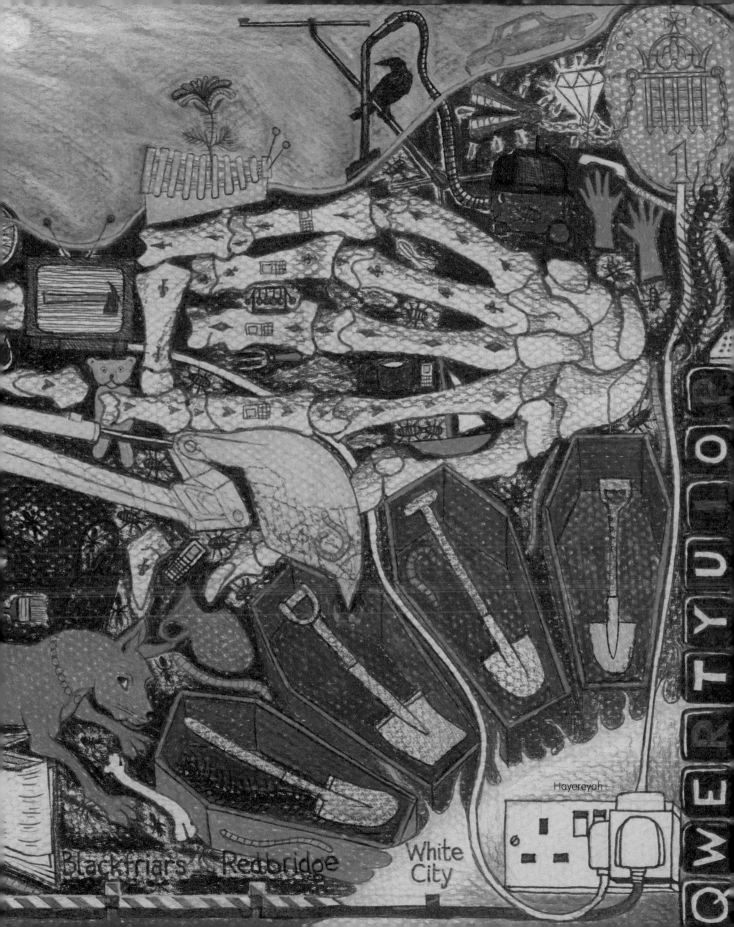

Blackfriars Redbridge White City

Hayereyah

Adrian Fleet

Jess Wilson

Laurie Storey

Katie Green

NATURE = HEALTH

TEMPLE OF GAIA

N A T U R E

community
community
community
community
community
community
community

MIGRATION ISTHMUS

RECYCLEDOM

ISLE OF CITIES

CARETAKERS

Compassion
Present   Future
Health

Lauren Towner

Nikki Pinder

Yoko Furusho

WELCOME TO INDIA NOW

words } and photography * Amelia
fonts ‡ David Chivall
with thanks to Ajay at Laxya Models
www.laxyamodels.com
and Rajat and Sanjana at Shanti Home, the delightful Bollywood themed hotel where I stayed in Delhi
www.shantihome.com
and Canon for the camera
www.canon.co.uk

TAXI DUO

Taxi Duo, bespectacled flop-haired Suman Samajpati and the taller long-faced Sourav Roy Chowdhury, met at school and have known each other for fifteen years. They have travelled 1500 kilometres across four states by train to be with me in Delhi, but appropriately enough they thoroughly enjoyed the journey, relishing the opportunity to collect new research material for their art. "Our name complements our art, which is all about creating a fantasy world, journeying into different lifestyles and motifs." They describe the trip with glee...

Suman: Of course it was fun! We always prefer to travel by train, moving and snapping out of the windows and meeting with the common peoples. From state to state there are very different cultures and the languages and food in the stations changes, which is fun – although English is always the same.
Sourav: And the further east we travel the greener it gets; in Bihar the soils are red which is very dramatic. Many poets, novelists and painters are inspired by the landscape of Bengal.
Suman: We always keep one small camera with us because different lifestyles and concepts are very important to our storyboards, but sometimes it's difficult to snag the images so we miss a lot.

We peruse the images taken on their camera the day before, and discuss the most inspiring sights. Perspectives offered by signal lights and trainlines get the Taxi Duo thumbs up, as do the gorgeous fields of feathery cream kash reeds emblematic of Durga puja, the most important Bengali festival. I feel like a total pleb as they describe how the celebrated filmmaker Satyajit Ray made extensive use of the same billowing white seed heads in his seminal film Song Of The Road, which is a visual love poem to the landscape of rural Bengal. Against a backdrop of kash small boys gambol, kite-flying. Many other sights inspire a poetical artist's interpretation from the Duo. "This brick burner in a field looks like an installation!" exclaims Sourav excitedly, zooming through the pictures saved onto his memory card. "And here's another." He points to a stand of trees isolated in stark relief against the skyline within a field. "In the Durgapur industrial area there are many installations." Inspiration it seems, is everywhere.

Sourav: We started this project together in 2005 but it is all getting going this year. I am a photographer and Suman is an artist. I was working at an advertising agency but I left earlier this year. This is absolutely better; much more freedom.
Suman: I had my first solo exhibition in 2000 in Bangladesh but the medium was very different. I used to paint abstract geometrical forms in acrylics and oils, but now we are exploring something new and different.
Sourav: We share common thoughts on art. We found an old portrait studio in Kolkata that was retouching photos, so we started researching photo-paintings which involves using oils, inks and dust colours on top of photos.

They will stay for only one day in Delhi, but have arranged to see the gallery that will be putting on their next show, the Religare Arts Initiative. Once open this huge 10,000 square foot space will be India's largest gallery. This will be Taxi Duo's fourth exhibition, following two previous ones in Delhi and one as part of a group show on South Asian perspectives on gender held in the Lincoln Centre in New York. Would they ever consider moving to the epicentre of the Indian art scene?

Both: Not at all!
Suman: Delhi is much more liberal, so it is easier for us to get good reactions here, but our families are in Kolkata and we are used to the style and the environment there. Delhi has another famous artist couple, so we are under pressure to be successful too!

Taxi Duo's photo-paintings are inspired by the works of middle eastern artists Lehnert and Landrock, Van Leo, and their contemporary Youssef Nabil, as well as most notably Pierre et Gilles. "We studied their works, but the technique is very secret to everyone and it is very difficult to get help or advice," says Suman, "we once wrote to Pierre et Gilles but we didn't get an answer!" Working together can of course have its challenges.

Suman: We have very different natures. When I am getting the storyboard and props together Sourav will be always asking if I am finished. I close the door but he waits outside making a noise!
Sourav: The reason we quarrel is because I say stop but he always says 'little more do!' [when I am retouching]. Everything is handcrafted in our studio.
Suman: Only we hire a professional make up man from the Kolkata film studios.
Sourav: And we hire professional film lights – we shoot only with direct light for dramatic effect on an obsolete Russian Kiev camera. We don't like very much digital cameras.

Each artwork takes more than two weeks to create, and if something goes wrong then they must go back to the beginning. Starting with clear ideas in mind they have spent up to a year searching for the right character to photograph.

Suman: It is very difficult to get a European or Mediteranean look in Kolkata. Eventually we find a fashion student who is also a model – he is not so good looking but he's having a very beautiful impression. He is always coming around to ask when he can do more work for us!
Sourav: He is a narcisistic character who can be both feminine and masculine, so we let his features do the talking.
Suman: We are very inspired by the underground filmmakers Jack Smith, Kenneth Anger and Derek Jarman. We use derivative decoration from Indian films and calendars but we want to have fun and challenge misconceptions so we use many effeminate androgynous characters. In old traditions these things (sexual mores) were talked about but now there is a huge vacancy in the art world. Many Indian artists of our generation are doing this work with sexuality. We are much more

free so there is an outpouring.
Sourav: We are too much bold in what we think!
Suman: Sometimes [our work] is intentionally homoerotic, sometimes not. The Blue Land series features a girl in reverse to show a different way of looking at women... you could find a lesbian idea here, in respect of the girl being surrounded by blue colour to show masculinity.
Sourav: But our next project will be about the different cultures, lifestyles and rituals of city life in Bengal. We will shoot at the holy city of Varanasi on the banks of the Ganges.

The hyper-real photo-retouched style that Taxi Duo have adopted is perfectly suited to Indian culture, no more than a step away from much of Bollywood's imagery.

Suman: People say our images are very reminscent of traditional film posters, and in particular one that has just come out, but the film was released after we made the artwork. Sometimes old actors made the same kind of movements our models make for the camera, like playing with butterflies.

Sourav: We like to break concepts and we are very liberal. We make very high camp Hindi style!

Despite skirting around the question several times I am still no clearer as to whether Taxi Duo are a couple, although I am fairly convinced they are. I ask once again and Suman chuckles. "We are not at all gay! We are gender liberal; in school we all mix together and we have lots of girlfriends and boyfriends... but a lot of people say we are gay." Of course it doesn't really matter, but so much of their work seems to focus on the liberalisation of gender mores that it does seem odd that they are so non-commital. "We are not doing any campaign, we are just part of a liberal generation that wants to cross all dogma," Sourav affirms. Taxi Duo – up for pushing boundaries and challenging the traditional status quo, but not quite clear, at least to my perception, on their own desires. It may yet be early days for the sub-continent's own Pierre et Gilles, but I suspect they are destined to become the hottest new darlings of Indian contemporary art.

MIDIval PunditZ

MIDIval PunditZ is Gaurav and Tapan, both in their early thirties and the first Indians to sign an international deal for contemporary music – with Six Degrees, a San Francisco based record label. "They have never been to India but they are awesome people." Embracing classical Indian music, drum 'n' bass, trance, bhangra and rock, their name is a reference to their higher caste Brahmin (priest class) backgrounds, "the punditz are here!" and the technology used to create their music. Sid, who does "the legwork" for their Indian record company, meets me in his father's car to whisk me through Delhi to Tapan's apartment in the upscale Greater Kailash area.

"We're currently working on our third album, and we'd love Storm Thorgerson to do our artwork," says Tapan, lifting a heavy tome of Storm's famous album covers for the likes of Pink Floyd and Audioslave from the table and flicking through the glossy pages. Following behind him into his black-walled home studio, I am subjected to a blast of bassy house that is radically different to the band's previous fusion recordings. "Break that, shake that, take that, digital boy / Break that, shake that, take that, digital girl" goes the droning vocodered voice. With barely an Indian musical reference this would not sound out of place in a big western nightclub. It's clear that, having travelled the world, MIDIval PunditZ are setting their sights on a whole new audience. "This album is a departure."

"We pioneered our own club nights back when noone else was doing it," says Tapan. Ten years ago the nascent MIDIval PunditZ were fresh out of college, where Tapan studied engineering and Gaurav studied architecture. Intent on providing a forum for the kind of music they wanted to hear, they set up their now legendary Cyber Mehfil nights, the meaning once again a combination of the old and the new – Cyber in reference to the internet and Mehfil after the Urdu word for a gathering of artists. They had five hundred people at the first party. "We knew that people were bored so there was a lot of excitement. It became a cult event and people started to bring along their own visuals and CDs to play." To promote their events MIDIval PunditZ use couriers to deliver flyers. "They're really cheap and can tell us that a flyer has been received. We also find that SMS messages work very well because they are so personal." Sometimes Tapan will call as many as two hundred people to tell them about a gig. "I don't get into a long conversation but it's a great gesture! It makes our fans feel they know who we are." The canny PunditZ boys will use whatever they can to promote their music – MySpace and Last.fm provide great forums whilst Facebook has become hugely important in letting young Indians know about social events.

At this point Tapan's male helper arrives home, followed shortly by both Gaurav and Tapan's fiancée Anoushka, a tiny, trendy girl who is a fashion photographer. I am offered a cup of tea. "We're very spoilt. I never make my own tea, which is really hard to get used to when I go abroad. I'm not proud of it but it's not my fault." The massive reliance on domestic servants is something that I still find hard to grasp. "I hate doing laundry and making coffee and tea," affirms Gaurav. "We're lucky to have certain luxuries." I question whether Anoushka will be able to continue her career if they have children. "Of course – she will have help. I have friends who have two maids for one child. My mother was a university lecturer and the maid fed us because she worked."

MIDIval PunditZ moved quickly on from doing remixes to making their own music. "Remixes have a short shelf life. You won't even get the publishing rights! It's totally not yours." In 2003 they were invited to tour America as part of the Return of the Asian Massive tour, and they returned recently to Brooklyn to do a live performance in front of a large projection of the Bruce Lee movie Enter The Dragon. Last year they played on the Jazz World stage at Glastonbury. "The English are a tough crowd; they get bored easily and think you are self indulgent if you play long solos." Was it raining, I ask, remembering the god-awful deluge of 2007. "Yeah, it was! The rain was falling in my beer but I was still drinking it!" Tapan seems much amused by the vagaries of British festival etiquette. He saw The Who, Bjork, The Chemical Brothers and the fabulous Rodrigo y Gabriela, who made a lasting impression. "We got to meet them backstage and they're super cool. I'd like to get them over to India." British crowds are a source of constant amusement – at the Custard Factory in Birmingham they played to a packed "totally desi" British Asian crowd. "They were all nicely dressed, like a date situation; gel, cologne, everything. But then they became all disgusting, with the make-up falling off. So much energy! They can break straight into Hindi or Punjabi but they have this funny accent and they say 'innit' all the time! It's all they say!" he recalls amusedly. They have also toured in, erm, Austria. It's a good thing they are happy to play to both an Indian crowd and a mixed audience. "There is a very different reaction from a predominantly white crowd; they react more emotionally because they don't understand the words."

Licensing is a major source of income for MIDIval PunditZ, who have contributed a song to the hit series Six Feet Under, as well as to the soundtrack for the film Monsoon Wedding. "We are in the loop for the 'Asian exotic' sound. We'd love to score a whole movie one day." Most MIDIval PunditZ songs steer away from the personal because "it is traditional in the languages of the north to sing in the third person, and we've always had to deal with the weight of Bollywood which is formula driven, situational," says Gaurav. Fortunately there are now many younger directors and scriptwriters who are open

to bolder choices for their scores. One of the boys' newest tracks mixes English and Hindi lyrics together in the same song for the first time; two different male voices, recorded separately, call to each other in a highly personal song about loneliness. "What is lonely? Everyone is lonely sometimes..." says Tapan.

Before the light fades we head onto the rooftop to take a photo. It's all going swimmingly when we are interrupted by a phonecall to tell us that several bombs have gone off across central Delhi; one extremely close to where we are – Gaurav is convinced he heard it. Racing down the stairs Tapan flicks on the enormous telly in his bedroom and for the next ten minutes we are glued to the images of bloodied bodies flashing up across the screen as everyone speculates on the cause of the attacks. And then it is time for me to leave, to make my way home across a 'metro city' in a state of emergency.

Neelangan Ghosh works in a residential backwater, down a dusty alley past some recently built but abandoned commercial buildings; the kind that now criss-cross Delhi due to new zoning restrictions put in place by the government in the run up to the Commonwealth Games. Originally from Kolkata, Neel has lived in the area since arriving to study at the National Institute of Fashion Technology seven years ago. As he darts back and forth in the cool blue-washed basement studio to talk with his workers, we catch up on the history of his label.

Neel is one of the first people I interview in Delhi and I am still at the stage where I am surprised by the number of qualifications he has. A first degree in engineering – specialising in aerodynamics – led not

deadlines often have to stay far longer than the allotted hours and are constantly at risk of being poached – is clear in his dealings with them. "Everyone in the design community knows who the good embroiderers are. Their skills are passed down the generations and they are very valued. A lot of dirty stuff happens..." Yet Neel's workers prefer to stay with him than return to the often horrendous conditions in the export houses, even when finances have been especially tight and the pay sometimes late.

Neel showed his collection for the first time this April and was quickly snapped up by the chic designer store Kimaya, which stocks over one hundred new Indian designers and has stores in Delhi and Mumbai, as well as Dubai. "From exclusive

make them stand out in the crowd, but nothing too outrageous. "There is a lot of bling happening, you can say! And you have to use a lot of embroidery."

We look through the current collection, which involves lots of bulky beaded embroidery on shiny fun-coloured satin fabrics cut in young swing shapes, and Neel confesses that he had wanted to do some exciting things with silhouettes and buttons, but decided to instead produce what the market wants. So he based his debut collection around the concept of old people's homes! "I try to address social, moral and global issues," he says. "I believe that designers should address important issues [in their work] because of the media presence that can be used to spread a message." This

NEELANJAN GHOSH

to a glorious career but to a teaching post in Bangalore. Sensible studies over, he applied for a design degree. "I had always worn fancy clothes, so I wanted to put my skills to something better," he explains. "Of course, my background helps with the technical stuff such as cutting patterns." NIFT Delhi is considered the best of all the regional colleges and the competition to secure a place is stiff. "I had a real passion for fashion, but many just want an easy way into a glamourous world. They are unprepared for how much hard work it is." Graduating in 2004, he set about securing loans and finding skilled workers with which to start his own label, which finally took off last year. The mutually respectful relationship that he has with his staff – who on

designer wear to chic accessories to enhance your look with, Kimaya will leave you looking your gorgeous best," gushes the flashy website. "Indians have become much more aware of fashion," he says. "Five years ago only the rich were buying high fashion, but now travel is cheap so people are curious about what there is out there; they travel in India and go to Europe. Plus younger people are getting paid very well so my designs are pretty affordable for them." He is realistic about the need to cater for the festival season, which is a big market for the domestic fashion industry. "There are so many festivals, practically every day! And the marriage season gets into full swing in October." Customers want a nice fusion of styles for these events: something to

means that he has employed traditional embroidery techniques to portray the antiques that modern India is so eager to collect and consume, whilst at the same time neglecting elderly family members – that which is most precious of all. Cards, elaborate picture frames, vintage telephones and cars, big old alarm clocks – all have been tackled by Neel's embroiderers, who regard the unusual motifs as a creative challenge. "Wisdom is not revered in the same way it once was," he complains animatedly. "Everyone is getting too busy to look after their parents, so they send them away to old age homes and forget about them." He assures me that this is not the case in his family. "But it's part of the modern busy lifestyle, where people want to do things

model)(Samyukta at Laxya Models

their own way in a smaller nuclear family." Property prices in the cities don't help, for it is often too expensive to house extended family. Naturally he realises that buyers are unlikely to pay much attention to his ideas, but were the media interested in hearing about his concept in the end? "No, they really don't care, but I feel good about it."

The beaming Rajul has recently joined Neel to help shoulder some of the weight. "I've got so much to do but I don't want to devote all my time to admin so now we are sharing the responsibilities," he explains. Rajul is positively bouncing with the thrill of her new role, far away from the commercial job she left behind in Mumbai. "Creatively it's very enhancing to work as a combination and it's lovely to see the pieces taking shape as I think of them." They explain their latest plan to split the business into two labels. Neel's current label will become the premier 'bling' line catering to what the Indian market wants, and a new 'sub-label' named Strip Poker will be launched next year. "I want to do much more creative funky stuff. Strip Poker will be more colourful, younger, more experimental. It's always 'oh you do Indian stuff' or 'you do western designs', but fashion is getting more global so I want to do something that anyone can wear anywhere." Strip Poker will allow them to indulge their more outrageous aesthetics. "Our motto is more is more... we love layering and we don't know when to stop!" they laugh.

Neel and Rajul excitedly show me a fabulously over-the-top piece that they are working on. The heavy sequinning calls to mind Ashish, one of my favourite designers, but the words on the huge starry vodka bottle are all Neel's own. Spelling out Neil Armstrong, they are a jokey reference to Neel's nickname amongst friends, and a statement against the fickle celebrity culture of India. Based on "how everyone wants everything," Neel will again use the medium of fashion to comment on contemporary culture, and more specifically the desire to attain short-lived starry status with the aim of making money from commercial endorsements. He tells me about the rifleman who gained a medal at the last Olympics but failed to even place at this one. "With one acheivement he became like a demi-god but the hype was completely over the top because it was not justified," he says. "The shooter was too involved in partying and social functions to do any practice." I think of the huge poster campaign featuring the rifleman that I see on my daily commute into central Delhi. "These people will put their names to anything and everything: mustard, soup..." In an ironic gesture of disparity, Neel will soon be doing the same. With his name, on his clothes.

PRATIBHA

Pratibha lives in one of many new housing blocks that are springing up on the far south side of the saved Delhi forest. We scamper onto the roof to take a photo, and I look out in awe at the remains of many ancient temples peeking above the unexpected expanse of greenery. Pratibha is short-haired, impish, bouncing with an intense energy as she skids around her small flat full of family, friends and the small children of neighbours.

But she wasn't always so at home with people. As a child growing up home-tutored in Iraq Pratibha led a sheltered and insular life. "Dad was very angry and very strict. He didn't know how to express himself and was overwhelmed by the experience of having children; he couldn't give or receive love. Mum had no time for me even though we had no neighbours or friends." When the Gulf War forced them home to India thirteen year old Pratibha found it hard to cope with the busyness, the dust everywhere, the sensory overload. "It was so different," she remembers. "In Iraq the roads were empty for miles, and I had been happy in my own internal world of images. I was sick in bed for a year [when we returned]."

Her innate creativity sent her to the "very competitive and very professional" NIFT to study garment design, but it was "not passion fashion" and she struggled to be inspired until one day a kind man told her about Dali, whom she studied with fervour. "Chailash was the only person who spoke to me, and now he's my husband." I glance over to where a smiley man plays dotingly with their small son on the sofa. Her final college collection paid reference to Dali's disappearing object – designed to be viewed under UV light, forms and shapes would disappear and reappear. For a few years she worked in the manufacturing industry before starting her own label creating digital printed t-shirts and bags in 2004.

Pratibha and her husband moved into their apartment three years ago and shortly after she fell pregnant by him, "this man" as, strangely, she refers to him. She was not happy, and candidly tells me that she was on anti-depressants during this period. "I was going through so many emotions," she explains. "I felt

we had an inbalance over [our opinions of] love and life, and I had become close to a junior graduate called Darshan at NIFT who would share all his work with me. I could see myself in his sketches and we became really close; nothing was said or done but I had all these really amazing feelings." Matters came to a head when she had a vision of herself rising out of the earth and walking up a ramp surrounded by children. Darshan, despite obligingly sketching from Pratibha's tale, would not show her the outcome, which left her hurt and confused. "When I came home something was really broken inside. But I realised that it

was really important for me to start doing my own sketches. So I took the same book and pen that he used and began to draw my feelings." She found that she had drawn a foetus, "as if I was feeling a child in my life." Things took a stranger turn still. "I could sense this 'Jesus energy' all around me, as though I had conceived a child right at that moment." She went for a test but it was negative. "I thought; I am pregnant, but my son is hiding from me." She felt tired, heavier, and was involuntarily signing all her drawings with the name Yeshwa (meaning Jesus) rather than Pratibha. At three months her pregnancy was finally confirmed and despite her initial worries that "being a mother means in a way that your life is over so I wasn't looking forward to it," she felt suddenly light. "I felt an intense craving for my own personal space, so I started to withdraw from my [fashion] studio. I didn't want to be near anyone, and sat for hours every day sketching in the corner of my bedroom." She suddenly cut off all her long hair because "I had been quite prepared to become a dignified and graceful mother but then I thought, 'I'm really not in that phase. I feel more like a warrior at this time in my life.' So I asked my hairdresser to make me look like how I felt."

In a rapid-fire stream of consciousness Pratibha gives me a guided tour through her entire first sketchbook, a love story for her unborn son. "It was as if Yeshwa was making his own patterns; writing his own book. I could feel his soul coming into life." She put on weight and began to draw more curves and pendulums in response. "I had always been a careful eater and now I wanted to experience eating without thought, so I became huge." Wombs, nests, "alien friends", birds and bees "like construction workers on a construction site" populate her intricate pen drawings. Even her breasts become the subject of one sketch, intrigued as she was by their changing nature. "This is when I was due to deliver any day," she says as we near the end of the book, "it looks like a 'phuljhari' – a firecracker we use at Divali. It was how I felt, ready to explode." It suddenly occurs to me with absolute clarity that Pratibha is a synaesthesic. Everything that she has described about her life is visually, orally overwhelming. From her need to escape the overpowering reality of Indian street life to her dramatic sensory awareness of her body, it seems obvious. For a second, I stem her tide of explanations to describe my theory, but she has never heard of synaesthesia, so we do a quick Google search together and she is intrigued by how accurately it describes her life. "I look around and think 'how come other people don't feel like I do?' but maybe they just don't experience it. I thought that everyone was keeping a secret from me!"

Throughout her pregnancy Pratibha did not see Darshan, but in the ninth month they met up. "He was so shocked [by my changed shape] and couldn't stop laughing as he held my stomach. It was like a reunion with part of my soul." I question whether all her drawings were made with Darshan in mind.

Was she trying to impress him? "Maybe," she concedes. "I always imagine what his reaction would be. I was projecting onto him because I so wanted to experience that level of pure feeling that he seemed to have. I never know what my husband thinks; our conversations never seem to go anywhere. For awhile I felt that it was all over and I was only capable of living through art." At Pratibha's suggestion she and Chailash sleep at opposite ends of the apartment, but appear happy together in my presence; in fact she acknowledges that her husband, in the process of changing from son to husband to father, has held the family together and they are now "coming out of the confusion." Whether he will ever return to the marital suite is unclear.

Even as she went into labour Pratibha could not stop drawing, and laughs that her first official exhibition was a "labour table show" with everyone in the hospital stopping by to see the crazy lady sketching her way through the pain. When Yeshwa arrived he was as she had dreamt him to be. "I had a vision of carrying my father in a pram through ruins when I was a child. My son is just like him." For the first three months Yeshwa had colic and things were far from easy. Used to her independence, Pratibha felt trapped. "I had always needed someone there, but now I felt free of the need for others' opinions." She swapped her ink pen for the paintbrush and set about creating a number of bold paintings – bearing names like Golden Womb and Sex – to describe how her relationship to her body has changed. "I don't know what I'm doing," she confesses "but I don't want to stop this. I had lost my identity and it's the only thing that keeps me alive. It is such a strong experience for me, like making love with art. I feel very peaceful and healed when I paint." Pratibha now signs her own name. "This painting almost killed me," she exclaims, pointing to the Van Gogh inspired The Spaceship. "I got so engrossed in circling every little dot, each representing every little particle from here to the last dust of creation, all filled with love." Some of her artwork has also been translated onto delicately embroidered canvasses by that most useful of Indian resources, skilled craftsmen.

I discovered Pratibha by luck – through a recommendation, for she has not had time to market herself properly and has never exhibited any of her art. "Artists become very decorated in India, but for me this is not a

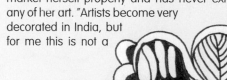

career option. I did not choose to do this, I just have to do it. It is the only way I am able to live – watching my baby and painting all day." She has no intention of emulating her own mother's hands-off approach, "so I want to know every expression on my baby's face." And she is adamant that Yeshwa will be the only one so that she can concentrate on her work. The children racing around us clearly appreciate Pratibha's light manner. "I love having them in the house and they love the freedom. They can paint wherever they want. I have no rules." At toddler height the flat is a riot of scribbles. Before I met Pratibha I was able to view her work on the influential India Art News website, which offers a virtual community for artists. "If they feel my work then they will come to me, but for many it is hard to understand that I live my life through my art," she says. "There is only one artist in Delhi that I can share my feelings with... but I don't actually like his work."

Pratibha is currently obsessed with sacred geometry and the notion of prophecies. "Everyone is subconsciously following the same principles. Even respected physicists are talking about what the Bible, the Mayans and Sirians have said. Everything is happening in parallel." She believes that we are just part of a particular phase of life, heading for ascension to a higher level. "I find it hard to cope with all the science, but we become what we think about. The universe is here because we have imagined it into existence." She aspires to the creation of something tremendous and everlasting: "I'd like to create something immortal like a rose window [often seen in medieval cathedrals]. I don't believe in coming and going. I believe in being – which is a very Indian concept."

And what of her relationship with Darshan? "Last time I met him he was working as a costume designer on a movie. He asked me to be an extra as a favour, but it was an awful experience. We were in some bloody jungle, Yeshwa was really uncomfortable, and we couldn't get out. I realised then that he takes me for a ride every time, so I erased him from my life and my phone." Determined to live exactly as her awesome and often challenging feelings dictate, Pratibha is a formidable woman. "I will die if I do something my heart says 'no' to. I can't compromise," she affirms. "I have to live according to how I feel."

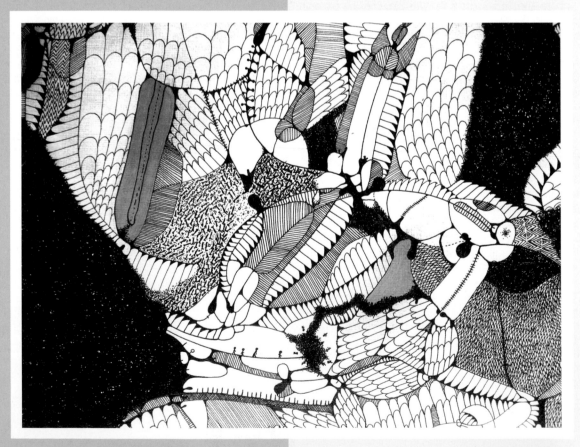

RAVI AGARWAL

The sun is setting as I arrive at the well appointed house in a gated community where Ravi Argwal lives with his ageing father. Smiling beneficiently, he welcomes me in and ushers me up to his top floor apartment, where he hands me a copy of his wonderful self-published book Immersion Emergence – in which he describes how the river Yamuna that flows through Delhi held him enchanted for two years. "I came to the river to find a quiet space where I could rediscover myself after a traumatic relationship," he says, but his yearning to cope with a deep personal crisis turned into a wider need, to "rediscover my roots in an increasingly changing city, [and] to recover my sense of self [in light of] the alienation I felt all around." The river holds a timeless quality; immovable, implacable, that Ravi finds

soothing. "Although it flows it somehow stays still. I am intrigued by the time beyond our short lives." A series of strangely discombobulating photos show him standing, shrouded, by the river; for "immersion has a multi layered meaning for Hindus." These powerful images are a meditation on Ravi's wish to be reborn during this life. During his wanderings along the river banks he discovered that the Indian government was poised to clear 40,000 families from the land to make way for a middle class enclave complete with golf courses, so he set about documenting their disenfranchisement. The city has decreed that the river should be sanitized "on the lines of the Thames," as part of a wider plan to 'clean up' Delhi in advance of the Commonwealth Games. God forbid that we are held up as a justification for mass population cleansing. "The city is gripped in its new imagination... waiting to join the likes of London and New York. Was the river being cleaned of its sewage or was the land merely being reclaimed for the city's powerful new middle class?" he questions.

It should not, perhaps, come as a surprise to discover that Ravi has long been involved in environmental activism, and in fact it transpires that he will be travelling to Senegal the day after I meet him, to receive an award in recognition of his ecological work. "It's nice to know that you're not working in isolation and that people care about what you do," he comments. "To some people I seem completely obtuse!" I imagine that he has done more than a little to rile the city's developers over the years, for thanks in no small part to Ravi's dedicated activism eight thousand hectares of forest in the centre of Delhi was saved for perpetuity in the early 90's. "Now it's legally protected and you can't touch a blade of grass in it," he says proudly. "Everyone said 'who can beat the development authority?' But I was the fool who rushed in!" Having studied both engineering and business studies prior to his art epiphany, Ravi was in a good place to put together a comprehensive research paper that included historical and technical information about the forest, before convening all the green groups whereupon they "held sit-ins, went on marches, mobilised school kids with a painting competition, got two films on national TV, sent postcards to ministers and wrote articles in the papers."

I ask if the campaigners held a big celebration when they learnt of their victory. "I don't feel we celebrate very much," he says a little wistfully. "We are quite a conservative culture." Ravi is obsessed by the nature of the city in which he grew up. "It's hard to get me depressed," he says "but I feel distant from the city. It's not happy, warm or personal anymore. The very fabric has changed – you are just a faceless somebody; nobody says hello in shops anymore. You could die in the street and noone would care. Other cities are more easy-going." In a new series he makes a mockery of our ridiculously bleak efforts to control and manage nature. Photos of elaborately manicured gardens are mirrored to emphasize their absurdity, and a bridge in the generic Japanese style is captured, incongruously planted on the lawns of a city park with not a drip of water in sight. "We feel so tense about chaos but only through chaos can we find something new; we don't like order but we can't find innovation," he tells me sadly.

His energies are now focused on the Trees For Delhi campaign. Because of the immense amount of construction work currently taking place, many beautiful old trees across Delhi are at risk of a brutal and sudden death. "Right now there is too much money [in this city]. It's a rich place now! People don't listen to reason, so it is hard to fight. They are promising a fast efficient city but to build the metro they are chopping down many trees. I say to them 'you stand for the roads but we stand for the trees.'" The developers now cut the trees down in the middle of the night to avoid the protesters, and Ravi goes out at 5am on most days to document the heartbreaking demise of the unlucky fallen ones for his Tree Memories project. Also captured by his lens are the 'bulldozer monsters' responsible for this mass extinction, squatly sat, dormant – like the toy transformers that were once so popular with children – as if to ridicule the childish decisions made by planners to 'improve' the city without respect for the environment.

In the past few years, in the newly invigorated contemporary art market, Ravi has been able to sell prints of his photos. "I blend all media and shoot both film and digital," he says, "what I choose is driven by my mood." He is entirely self-trained… "no art schools teach photography integrated with contemporary art. It is all very classical, but I like to shoot events, so my camera is always with me and I shoot all the time." For his series Ecology Of Desire Ravi slipped into the forest early in the morning after the monsoon rains. "Post monsoon colours are very intense and ethereal." He enters the forest alone, "privately, or people will otherwise think I am mad! It is a very meditative place to be." With the camera set on slow exposure he merges into the lush shrubbery around him. "It's about my own personal ecology, my relationship with the world around me. It is my responsibility to protect nature, for I am not separated from it. We survive together."

An avid birdwatcher since his early teens, Ravi's next public art project will highlight the plight of the humble vulture. Now, I've never been that keen on the concept of a vulture, but I will admit that my judgement was completely shallow, without consideration for their crucial purpose within India's ecosystem. "They are beautiful, clean birds who only eat dead bodies," says Ravi. The vulture population of India has crashed from 80 million in the 1980's to less than 10,000, but it took years for anyone even to notice that this once populous species was disappearing at an alarming rate. Eventually the cause was discovered; a cheap drug used by farmers on their cows was being consumed by the vultures when they fed on the cattle carcasses, resulting in rapid kidney failure. Recent studies suggest that the disastrous decline in vultures has led to a massive increase in rabies, spread amongst spiralling feral dog populations. "You no longer see vultures in Delhi," Ravi says mournfully, showing me a series of photos taken in 1980 when there were nests aplenty, dotted across the skyline. Efforts to enforce a ban on the offending drug have been painfully slow, and he jokes that "there are only two vultures left in the city, and they're stuffed." These lucky stuffed vultures will be shown on a large projection near the natural history museum where they now reside in perpetuity; constant reminders, thanks to Ravi, of our human folly.

menwhopause

An effusive and articulate bunch of laidback men in their late twenties and early thirties, menwhopause are my kind of people. I discover them nursing pints of beer in heavy glass tankards in Morrisons café, a rock joint situated unassumingly above plentiful jewellery and shoe shops in a scrofulous shopping precinct. They are many more in number than I am expecting, for menwhopause are an extended community, not just a band. "We are rock 'n' roll intellectuals!" grins the endearing guitarist Anup, introducing me to his flatmate Colin, a writer, and another good friend, the author Palash Mehrotra.

Their "commune", as they describe it, numbers up to twenty people and includes artists, filmmakers, a lawyer... and a dentist. "He's a friend who happens to be a dentist!" chuckles the garrulous Sarab; lyricist, husky voiced singer and advertising creative. On inspection their teeth are indeed absolutely impeccable. With no intention of signing to a large record company; "we got approached by EMI but the terms and conditions were shit," they have all the means to produce and distribute music in the way that they would like. "We have no deadlines: we're young, we're not in a hurry to make hit albums and rule the world!" laughs Sarab, blinking at me through his thick rimmed glasses. "We have the best band possible, we have no agenda! In advertising I have to work for clients, but the only time I am completely honest is when I am making music. I feel blessed to have met these guys."

menwhopause hail from six different states with typically diverse cultures, but they like to share celebrations – the entire band and extended community have just come from Anup's parent's house, where they enjoyed an eighteen course meal together in celebration of a Hindu festival. They all communicate across me in shotgun Hinglish, proud of their distinctive accent. Drummer Hemzi, who runs the Drum Institute, is a trained civil aviation engineer and devout Christian who doesn't drink or smoke. He's also forty years old, "I've had a long journey", with the dewy skin of a teenager. Sikh bassist Randeep, a photographer and interior decorator, is also teetotal, "he doesn't even eat eggs", and up until fairly recently had never even kissed a girl – in stark contrast to some of the band's antics. Sarab is a lapsed Sikh of Pakistani origin, "I love working in advertising," he says. "It's a way of life, just like music is. It is my absolute priority." Anup is not so keen on this newfound partnership. "He's beginning to love it a bit too much – he spends every night at the office," he complains. Yet they all agree that the band is the one thing that keeps them grounded. Ip, the acoustic guitarist, is also a non-practicing Sikh and somewhat fantastically the producer of a puppet show that satirizes Bollywood and politics on popular TV. "I got into it when I did music for some puppet shows in Rajasthan," he explains. "Music and puppetry collided. Now I have fun every day!" It is infinitely more rewarding than the job he held in a garment export house after completing a degree in carpet weaving, a skill that runs in the family.

The can-do attitude that prevails among Indian youth is exemplified in the meteoric rise of Anup – who, at twenty nine years old, is the youngest ever editor of Maxim. By all accounts this is a good job for a young man to have, entailing as it does a lot of drinking and hanging out with Bollywood totty. The band's manager, the gnomic Satish, pipes up, "Yes, he doesn't even introduce us to the models he knows, so selfish..." I am mightily impressed by the variety of interesting jobs the boys have. "What can we say?" laughs Anup. "We're just prodigies." But in reality they are incredibly grateful to the opportunities that, for the first time, have become available to their generation. "We try to do as much as we can," acknowledges Anup. This translates into sucking up every experience possible. "You don't have to sleep too much," decides Sarab, as he tries to persuade me to have another drink. "Once in awhile you can catch up – the night has not even begun yet." Competitive drinking has reached India. "We polished off four bottles of single malt last night," Anup tells me. "I drink at work!" Sarab rejoinders. The non-drinkers amongst them grin good-naturedly. I wonder out loud what has happened to the relaxed Indian lifestyle. "I've heard of it too... but who cares so long as you enjoy yourself," says Sarab, waving his hands around frantically.

Anup's roundabout career progress is intricately bound up in the formation of the band. "I studied chemistry at college, then I spent a year doing nothing with Sarab." Sarab was suffering an early career crisis too, so they hung out at his parent's house, where he was caught smoking weed on the balcony. "He got a lot of shit for it," says Anup. "It isn't accepted behaviour, but he marked his territory! For a year we did fuck all except listen to music and read books together." They would get trashed and practice, balancing a broken drum kit on the bed and testing out the bathroom for acoustics. Their first 2-track demo Fly Away was recorded at a now infamous rooftop party, and soon became a cult song, at least amongst their friends. Eventually the neighbours' complaints forced them to find a new rehearsal space, but, fortuitously by this time they had been joined by Randy, who was in the audience at their first official gig. "He sent us our first ever fan mail saying 'you're the band I've been looking for... can I come and hang with you?' It was straight from fan to band. He didn't even play the bass!" laughs the beaming Anup. The relaxed Randeep provided the nascent band with some much needed structure. "He's also the designated driver." Nowadays the band rehearse in a converted tailor's shop, courtesy of Ip's grandfather, and describe with unreasoned glee how it is out of action due to a termite infestation. When I visit the tiny space a few days later the air is heavy with toxic fumes, but I am impressed by how homely they have managed to make it.

"Eventually my girlfriend said she'd dump me if I didn't get a job," relates Anup. So he got a job working in one of the many export houses, but it really wasn't his style. "I was supposed to be harsh with the tailors so my boss got cross when I ate lunch with them or shared a samosa after work. I couldn't take it so I quit." He then enlisted Ip to hand out resumés at the studios where he was working, and got a job as features editor on The Pioneer newspaper, "a rightwing mouthpiece", where Satish was his boss. "The boom enables people to move easily across disciplines. We are very flexible," says Anup. Employers are looking for people with ideas, energy and a desire to work, so from conservative newspaper to babe-tastic bit of guff was an easy leap for Anup to make. And anyway, he only sees it as a stepping stone onto something else. In a quieter moment I discover that he has bought land in the mountains, and dreams of making a community there. Sarab, too, has plans for the greater good. "Advertising is at the root of all evil but I know what the solution is and I need to be in it. I'm doing non-advertising advertising!" He won't tell me what he means. "Just wait til I write a book," he smiles cheerily. "I want to occupy any and every space I can. I want to control your mind!" But more seriously: "You can't turn your back on what's happening every day, so you need to work on the inside to make a difference."

Entry to gigs is commonly free and by invite only, which means that most gigs are necessarily supported by advertising deals. "When we started there were no bands playing original music, so all the promoters said that people would be throwing rotten eggs at us," explains Anup. "But things have really changed in the past two to three years, and now it is really uncool to play covers." Although menwhopause are reasonably well known it has taken them a long time to get to this point. In 2007 Satish applied for a government grant so that they could travel to SXSW, fighting all the way for the right to export non-traditional Indian music. They are the first indigineous band to have played in the US and loved it so much that they self-funded a trip back to the festival this year, followed by a month long road trip from Texas to New York. "By the time we reached NYC we had no money left!"

Almost absentmindedly I ask how menwhopause got their name. "I can't believe it took you this long!" exclaims Anup. "I'm so tired of [the question], but basically I was in a quiz team at college and it was a stupid prank to call our team a double entendre." The name seems to have stuck. "We don't regret it," says Randeep. "Out of 1600 bands at SXSW we were in the top twenty five worst names so people will at least have heard of us." I am also curious as to why Anup's thumb is extravagantly wrapped up in bandages. "We have a new kitten named after the Bikini Killer, Sobhraj." He tripped over, jar of pickles in one hand and cat in the other. "So I had to make a choice about which I saved." By now Satish is thoroughly drunk, "like a baby" and veering periously close to my exposed cleavage with his camera. Instead of heading home as I had planned I end up accepting an invitation back to Satish's penthouse flat, where we lounge around on the balmy balcony – me and the Indian boys, swapping stories, playing with yet another kitten and eating expertly homecooked rice and dahl.

menwhopause: they take great delight in epitomising the new have-it-all over-achieving workaholic partying urban India, but are also lucky enough to be thoroughly grounded by the extraordinary friendships they have forged through their band.

GEORGE MARTIN PJ

I have arranged to meet George Martin PJ at his studio workshop behind the huge Hyatt hotel in the guts of Delhi. But he's late, or I'm early, and having been dropped off down a back street I find myself with half an hour to spare standing in a carpark/flytip next to a slum. A man sits cross legged in his makeshift stall and toothlessly offers me a cup of chai as the men who tinker in the brace of workshops close by eye me up lazily. I clutch my backpack close and hope I don't look as if I am carrying expensive equipment that doesn't belong to me.

George eventually arrives in a large car of the type that well-off artists around these parts drive – it is out of place down this dusty alley amongst the auto rickshaws and wandering cows. Gratefully I follow him down a narrow path into his sculpture workshop, wherein a workman is expertly carving an animal. We head upstairs to his huge airy painting studio (which is just below a similar one used by his artist girlfriend Rupa Paul) and he hands me an Appy juicy apple drink as we sit down at a makeshift table. It's hugely sweet and the moment I take my first sip I regret it – my teeth may well not survive this brief interview. He does not open his carton.

George is from the small village of Kochin in beautiful green Kerala. Being a Catholic descended from Anglo Indians he was given a very English-sounding name. Quaintly, his dad is called Joseph and his mother Mary – which should make him Jesus shouldn't it? He is one of a typically large family, which he believes has stood him in good stead. "People from big families are more committed and supportive of others." Now thirty four, George graduated from his college in Trivandrum in 1998 and moved to Calcutta to do an MA in fine arts before moving onto Delhi where he found work teaching sculpture at universities. By 2005 he was starting to gain recognition for his work and after winning "a big award" he now finds it "much smoother to make a living purely from art."

I first encountered George's artwork at the Palette Art Gallery, where a pair of sparkling grey sandblasted fibreglass monkeys faced each other enigmatically across a pair of virulent pink outsize molecules, in a piece entitled Smell Of Mute Mirrors. Since childhood George has been fascinated with "the poetry and mystery of fictional spaces" and his sculptural works often feature everyday objects that have fallen from their usual surroundings. The same installation features a huge glove of the type worn for washing up if you care more about your hands than I do. George is interested in the layers that humans build up as a buffer against reality. "The glove receives every experience first, so it is a sensual, intimate object... and then you throw it away." Poetry inspires George to reframe things. "The common stone on the road means nothing but if you throw it up in the sky it becomes more poetical. When I see a bed on the street I always ask 'what is underneath?' There is a darkness there that you can feel, and I want to illuminate that." He likens his work process to that of Magritte, and adopts a fairly obscure approach to the naming of artwork, saying that "meanings should be decided by the viewer: you set the stage, give them an opening to enter into the artwork [via the title] and then the interpretation is up to them." The questions raised by negative space are important; in Colourless Breath a goat is tied up on a table. "When a butcher slaughters an animal they first tie its legs and leave it in the street, which is far more shocking than the actual death." It is surrounded on all sides by keyhole cutout pulsating red walls – a direct reference to our sometimes uncomfortable voyeurism. He has been innovative in his installations in his use of recycled industrial materials and is now sought after by commercial sponsors such as Jindal Steel (which is constructing all the new bus shelters in Delhi) who would love him to promote their metals in sculptural form.

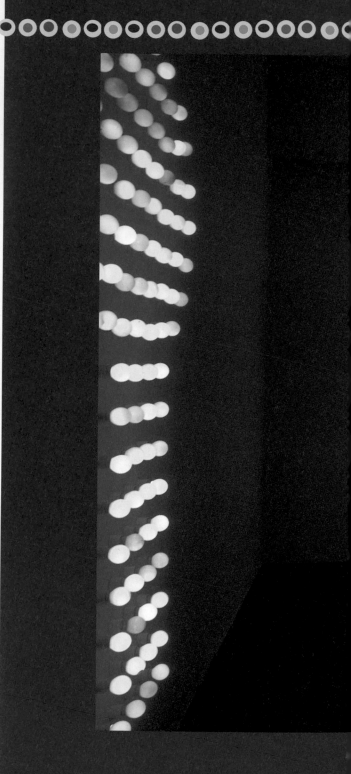

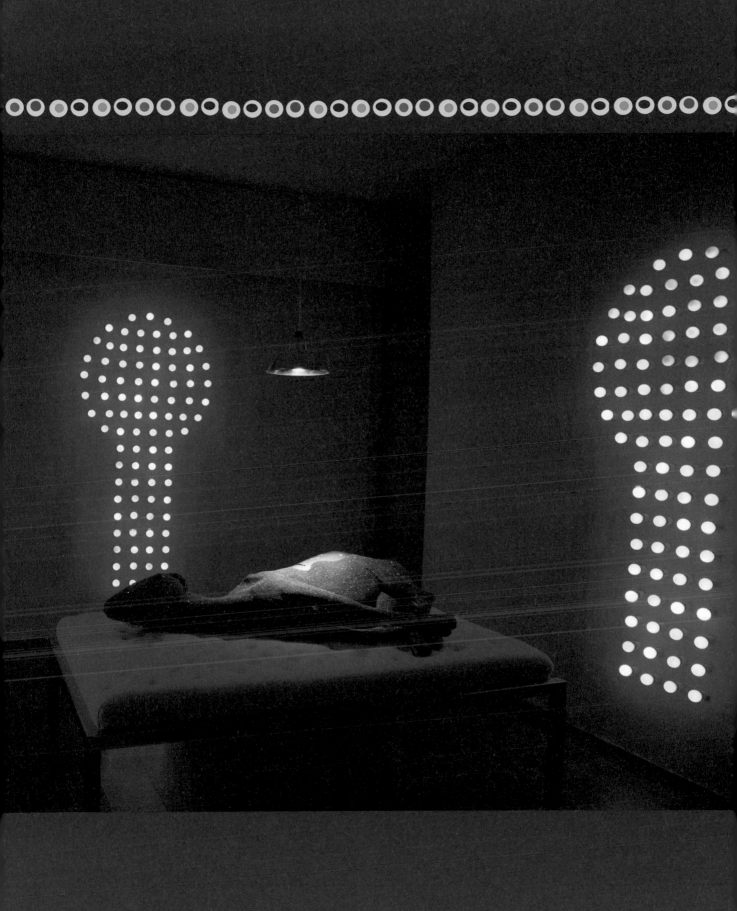

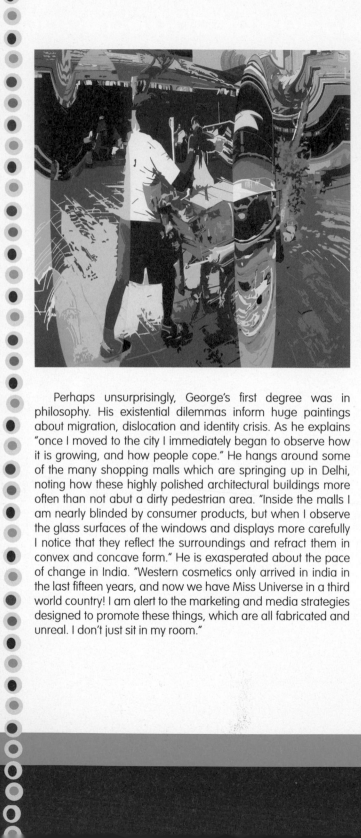

Perhaps unsurprisingly, George's first degree was in philosophy. His existential dilemmas inform huge paintings about migration, dislocation and identity crisis. As he explains "once I moved to the city I immediately began to observe how it is growing, and how people cope." He hangs around some of the many shopping malls which are springing up in Delhi, noting how these highly polished architectural buildings more often than not abut a dirty pedestrian area. "Inside the malls I am nearly blinded by consumer products, but when I observe the glass surfaces of the windows and displays more carefully I notice that they reflect the surroundings and refract them in convex and concave form." He is exasperated about the pace of change in India. "Western cosmetics only arrived in india in the last fifteen years, and now we have Miss Universe in a third world country! I am alert to the marketing and media strategies designed to promote these things, which are all fabricated and unreal. I don't just sit in my room."

George's paintings are searing in their intensity. "I am a little psychedelic in my mind," he chuckles. "My seniors at college all used 'pessimist colours' and I was not inspired. I liked more joyful vibrant colours then, and now." His judicious use of warm and cool colours creates unavoidable depth; sucking the viewer in to reconsider their environment afresh. Working across several canvases at a time he is sometimes forced to take a cathartic sculpting break from the physical brightness of his palette.

As well as making work for an upcoming solo show at the Vadehra Art Gallery George has some grand plans to create an artists' residency project for youngsters in his home village on land that he has already bought. "It's a nice place close to the river, a natural space," he describes. "Because the population is so high we keep spreading across the countryside, and nature is subjugated by us. But because education is getting better people are having fewer children, so things will change." Let's hope that doesn't also mean the loss of the compassion so often found in a large family.

model)(Nina Mishra at Laxya Models, location ÷ Shanti Home

NIMITA RATHOD

Twenty eight year old Nimita Rathod is one of the "most promising faces of 2008" according to the Indian media. She drives her small car full of clothes all the way across Delhi to meet me at my hotel.

Multiple studies

My first studies were in textile science, where I looked into the effect of chemicals on fabrics; I destroyed a lot in the process! ...but accidents can prove to be innovative. Once I realised that my interest was in fashion I went on to study at the National Institute of Design in Ahmedabad, Gujarat, where we were encouraged to work on projects with craftsmen in rural villages to help keep traditional crafts alive. I was then awarded a scholarship to do an MA in Milan, where I was able to work on full collections under the mentorship of international designers like Fiorucci and Rafael Lopez. I liked Italy because the people are very warm and family-orientated like us.

Setting up a label

An export design house that I was working for helped to finance the setup of my own label. I started with just a handful of people working for me but now I have a production unit in Gurgaon (a satellite town of Delhi) where twenty people work. My first show was at Lakme Fashion Week which supports a lot of young designers, but the sad part is that the government makes us pay entertainment tax on all our shows, which makes them very expensive. I have done two seasons so far but I am going to take a break from the catwalk until next March so that I can concentrate on building up a competent infrastructure for my business. Currently I sell in nine stores across India and to keep up with demand I have to produce a new collection every two months. In Delhi I stock in a shop called Aza in the Crescent Mall.

Inspirations for clothing

My first collection was created shortly after my return from Italy, where I fell in love with the way the buildings were dramatised by the effects of light and shadow. I liked the way that things were hidden, and then revealed, so I used colours and fabrics that reminded me of light and shadow. But I feel it is too early totally to define my look; with each collection I am trying to build on the one before and I am still exploring what I want to do. I like to play with the Indian sensibility for textiles so I work on concepts for unusual and interesting fabrics with traditional weavers. I also create couture looks for the festival season, which need a lot of shimmer and surface ornamentation.

Future plans

It is exciting because there is now such an immensely growing market in India. I would like to design home furnishings for my own label, but in the meantime I also design bed linen for the American firm Pottery Barn. In the long term, maybe I am being a little bit too ambitious, but I would like to work in association with an NGO to improve conditions for skilled craftsworkers.

www.nimitarathod.com

Them Clones are running late. As I nurse my paper cup full of tea in the generic coffee shop – part of a well-known international chain – a coterie of expensively dressed Indians shoot the breeze in the armchairs next to me. Eventually founder member Dev comes crashing in – he's come straight from his job, working in advertising. "I think I was hired primarily cos I'm in a band, so I must be cool and having creative thoughts." He is accompanied by new bassist Clarence; the others arrive in dribs and drabs as they get out of work. Despite national recognition and an army of fans, they are unable to make a living from music. "Them Clones was selected for the Great Indian Rock Festival for four years in a row which means that you have arrived," explains the soft spoken Clarence, whose father is of Portuguese origin. "Several hundred bands send in a demo but only the best twelve are selected. The first rock band that I ever saw was Them Clones at GIR in 2003 and they inspired me to get into music." In a span of eight years Them Clones has seen numerous line-up changes, mainly due to demanding careers. "We are a passion driven set-up," says drummer Dev. "We'd love to quit our day jobs but we can't, even though we're one of the top bands in the country. Only Hindi music from Bollywood actually sells anything; it takes 90% of the market share, and the remaining 10% is electronica and jazz. Even Britney doesn't sell and she's big here." Clarence and guitarist Gucci (pronounced Gooky) both do freelance music production for advertising and films, guitarist Joseph is an editor on a newspaper, and Dev's younger brother Prithwish sells televisions. "University is very strenuous here: there are lots of exams and it's getting worse every year, but once we 'passed out' [graduated] we spent a lot of time fooling around in our bedrooms," says Dev. "Our mum is very tolerant and supportive of us, although she always wanted us to have a career to fall back on."

Them Clones make populist rock of the type produced by middle of the road bands across the world. With a love for both metal and pop, they aspire to the mainstream. "We just write good hummable tunes," says Dev. "With rock riffs and pop melodies; we definitely aren't indie," clarifies Gucci. The band reflects the diverse ethnicity typical of Delhi, whose growing economy attracts Indians from across the sub-continent. "We're not limited by boundaries; there's just too many people [in India] so we spread where we can," says Prithwish. "We call Bengalis Bongs, and Joseph is a Chink," says Gucci, teasing the silent moon-faced guitarist from the north east. "Don't write that!" Joseph gives Gucci an unamused look. "When he disagrees he just looks at you..." laughs the cheeky Gucci, who is a beautiful Punjabi with shiny black hair, almond eyes and razor-edge cheekbones. "When we got independence they thought india would break up but it hasn't – there's unity in diversity," says Clarence. Not all is well though, as the divisions between rich and poor become more and more pronounced. "This is a very greedy environment where everyone is just running a business to amass cash for their own family," says Prithwish. "I have friends who've gone into the Civil Service for two years knowing that they can be corrupt and make lots of money, then leave. Even the prospect of jail doesn't put them off." This kind of thing has motivated Them Clones to write a song about being backed

into a corner. "It's like 'this is my space, get off my chest!' You let it out boss! We have some angry songs," exclaims Gucci. Despite a certain amount of disillusionment with the political climate, they are happy to accept the inevitable big brand sponsorship that enables them to play gigs.

In fact, Jack Daniels paid for Them Clones to visit London as part of a tour which also featured scuzz-rock band BRMC, of whom Gucci does not have a high opinion. "They insisted on playing their droning freakin' songs. We lost the will to drink even the free whiskey. Fuck it, we left." They were disappointed but not surprised by the feedback from the big labels they visited. "They all said 'sorry, but you need to have an Indian element, like a tabla'. Only Bollywood sells abroad," Dev says resignedly. They'd love to visit other big festivals like SXSW but are unwilling to take on such huge expenses until they have some new material to peddle. "We're a relatively lazy band," says Gucci. But their biggest obstacle, with eighteen songs written and ready to go, is finding someone suitable to produce their album. "It's a basic problem," explains Dev. "When we listen to other Indian [rock] bands there is always that wall of sound missing." The producers amongst them are more skilled at commercial work and don't feel up to the challenge. "We've spoken to fifteen producers both here and abroad but we just don't have the budget to hire someone really good." Luckily the situation has recently been resolved, and production of the next album is now imminent – with an Indian producer from New Zealand at the helm.

In the characterless mall the evening is getting on, so we venture out into the rain in search of somewhere to take a photo. Them Clones end up squatting unglamorously in the dirt beneath the red, green and white sign for a fast food pizza parlour. It isn't long before an interested crowd of men on mopeds surrounds us, somewhat unhelpfully blinding us with the intensity of their headlights.

THEM
CLONES

VISHAVAJEET DHIR

With the Stone Roses blasting from the small stack stereo in the corner, Vish describes how, at thirty years old, he has just returned from four years in Milan. With his shoulder length thick black hair, clip-cloppy brogues and well ironed shirt tucked into expensive jeans, Vish cuts a spectacularly Italian dash through the bustling lanes of Shahpur Jat. Growing up in rural Madhya Pradesh he developed an early love for beautiful things. "My parents taught in a boarding school in a really remote and desolate place, near the spectacular 8th century Gwalior Fort." We discuss the amazing natural air conditioning employed in the fort, which channelled cool winds over fragrant spices to create fresh sweet smelling air. "I was teased a lot at school," he remembers. "I got the brunt of my father's good education so he wanted me to get a good corporate job... my parents are a bit worried about me!" He shrugs in the resigned way of someone who is used to fighting his corner.

Like all good fashion designers Vish attended NIFT. "I studied business before fashion, so getting in was like a dream come true; it meant that I could do something with my life other than be a sales guy." On graduation he won an international design competition and took up a six month internship at the Diesel design studios in Milan, which he loved, "but I prefered Diesel when it was a bit more folky, like a jingle jangle band," he says. "It uncharms me now." I like his description: how apt. He then worked for various other studios but visa hassles eventually forced his return to India – trouble was, by this time he had a European girlfriend and a distinct love for all things Italian. "I miss my wine, weather, people in their best turn out," he laughs. "I love the food." Early next year he plans to marry his girlfriend, also a designer, "she's completely a high fashion girl" in Belgium. I am impressed that they are sustaining such a long distance relationship. "Baby, I'm running on faith! We speak a lot and I see her twice a year. I wouldn't be happy without her," he says, showing me a photo of them together on the pin board above the desk. She looks young, fresh-faced, with the bloom or 'bloss'

Before I meet with Vish he calls several times to find out whether I would like "champagne or tea" and on my arrival at his characterful flat in the poor textile district of Shahpur Jat I am presented with a delightfully presented cream cake on a little tray. Charmed by these little gestures, I set about sifting through his rail of clothes and soon discover that Vish is a total control freak. Determined to style and art direct every shot, he hangs off my shoulder with his nose up against the camera's digital screen until eventually my irritation drives him away. I am thankful when the shoot is over and we sit down to a lovingly laid out take-away "Chinese with an Indian twist" lunch in his bedroom-cum-studio.

on her cheeks after which he has named his label. He plans to move to Belgium; get a job there, or carry on production of his label in India. "I would rather move there – she likes the idea of India – incense, flowers – but for her the reality is not so cool..."

Vish's debut collection is based on a romantisized concept of an 18th century English tea party and is almost entirely white, with cleverly cut detailing of pastel patterning on biscuit. I can't help feeling that white is perhaps not the most sensible colour to wear in India but Vish begs to differ. "India is all about colour but in September most people feel like wearing white because it's so hot... and I love white," he explains, "but I'm not doing it again. It gets too dirty!" His first season was well received, yet the hard economic truth is that it is very difficult to sell this kind of design in India, where everyone wants a fancy ballgown. In an ideal India he would also produce menswear, notoriously even harder to sell. "I like my men to be really masculine," he says, looking distinctly effeminate, "like D-Squared, Brokeback Mountain, the lumberjack look."

Our delicious lunch finished Vish accompanies me out of Shahpur Jat, stopping momentarily amongst the toppling piles of mustard baby aubergines and livid purple tomatoes to help me purchase strings of multicoloured beads. As we commandeer an auto rickshaw on the street his parting words to me are "try and relax". Nothing is guaranteed to wind me up more. Towards the end of my stay he calls me again, this time to wonder why we haven't had time to catch up and do some more shopping together – it's a sweetly touching gesture and I am left pondering what a curious mix he is; a genteel and caring fellow yet with very little concept of boundaries and social mores. Maybe it will stand him in good stead, tackling the firmly delineated Indian world of fashion.

SUDHIR & TAPASH

words } Dearbhaile Kitt

Sudhir Nayak and Tapash Biswas have been friends since they met on the infamous fashion design course at National Institute of Fashion Technology in Delhi. Bonding over their shared outlook on fashion they graduated in 2002 and joined forces to design under their label Stae. After a couple of years of preparation; "it was important to have the proper production infrastructure in place first," their first a/w 08 collection has been shown to great acclaim. The pair are now based in their hometown of Calcutta: a deliberate choice borne out of a desire to support local textile craftworkers.

Setting out

It made sense to work together because we already had a firm friendship and knew each other's strong and weak points. But it has been a struggle to make it. When we first started out no one was really fashion conscious in India so there was only a small niche market. Things are improving now and we sell in thirty stores domestically, as well as many more abroad in South Africa and the Middle East.

Saris and western design

We were born into and brought up with a strong sense of traditional Indian culture and the sari is a strong representation of that: you can't overlook the needs of a whole generation. It was difficult at first to see the sari in a non-traditional way but we managed to design a new look for it and of course we also design for contemporary markets because India is changing rapidly and you must appeal to the younger generation. We try to make all our clothing both stylish and comfortable.

Artist's muse

For our debut a/w 08 collection we dreamt up a story about an artist who has creative block and is fed up with his painting style. He searches for inspiration and finds a beautiful muse who inspires him to start painting new work. The collection is based on the moment the artist finally starts to paint strokes onto the canvas again. We both find painting very relaxing and Sudhir actually hand painted all the pieces. Winter is a great season in India: we get to experiment with wearing lots of clothing, and it's the festive season!

Next for Stae

We are showing our s/s 09 collection soon and we are still both rather nervous about how our collections will be received by the market. We hope to gain more fans: maybe Sonia Gandhi [a prominent politician] could wear one of our saris, and we'd love to get Madonna in one of our contemporary designs. We'd like to take a short break if possible! Usually we only get time for a small nap whilst listening to some classical music.

model }{ Gauri Anand
location ÷ Shanti Home

MANIL GUPTA

Manil Gupta arranges to meet me at the posh Palette Gallery, a cool white space behind barred gates in the exclusive enclave of Golf Links. Managed and run by rich fashion designers Rohit Gandhi and Rahul Khanna the gallery aims to display the most unique contemporary art in India, and is clearly a key destination for the moneyed ellite of Delhi.

"In the last year I haven't shown much at all because I have been focusing on my work," says Manil, standing casually in jeans, t-shirt and flip-flops in the middle of the empty gallery, which is attended only by appointment. "I have been improving my vocab by removing all colour and emphazising the optical illusion effect. I decipher elements that narrate the human existence in relation to whatever I've gone through." We ponder one of his new large-scale black and white paintings, striped parts flying off in all directions. "These are mostly figurative works which are a hybrid of animals, humans and nature. I am interested in the exploitative aspect of human existence. we perceive ourselves as the highest chain of existence yet all we do is destroy." He tells me how the documentary Earthlings, narrated by Joaquim Phoenix, has profoundly affected his views "Joaquim talks about how we are totally reliant on animals and yet we have managed to exploit them all to further our own selfish interests. It's a bit gloomy but it's a fact I want to share with everyone." Manil saw the film earlier this year and it has informed all his work since. "It's like we're all going 'don't worry baby it's going to be alright' even though, as Al Gore said, we are now facing the consequences of our actions. But I have hope that we can step up to our place in existence. What we have is such a privilege and it's beautiful, but we must be more sensitive to one another." He worries that the human psychology justifies everything for human interest, for example "what qualifies some species to be endangered when others are not? You kill this, you kill that... so it's all the same. Death is relative but pain is not so you need to be sensitive, and if we are able to be sensitive to a 'lower being' then we'd be better off with ourselves."

Manil's paintings hold the viewer's attention through their bold execution, which reveal their meanings only when contemplated for awhile. "I try to find a balance in my life and I think I find it through my art, which allows me to look at the bigger questions and attempt to find the answers," he says. "And I think it is important to put those questions out there." But the art market is scared of anything negative, preferring instead "flowery, pleasing, hanky-panky art." I love this description but worry that I have heard Manil incorrectly. He assures me that I did not, which pleases me greatly – Indians often come out with such fabulous turns of phrase.

Both male and female forms are given equal space in Manil's paintings. "There are no gender issues here! I treat both equally," he assures me. I discover that gender issues are a big deal to the intellectual classes, with much energy expended by women trying to regain control of the male gaze; a problem very specific to Indian culture. "Artists are good at relating to the human struggle and although we are a great developing nation, bursting onto the world, it is struggle that still informs the lives of the majority." The Indian media adopted the slogan 'India Shining' to describe the modern age a few years ago, but it was hugely unpopular amongst the vast majority of citizens since only a handful are reaping the rewards of the economic boom, faltering as it is these days. Because many successful artists like Subodh Gupta (who shares the Palette Gallery but is now too busy to talk to the likes of me) are from rural areas, it is easy for them to romanticise the struggles. "He is from a very humble background and worked his way up," says Manil, as we look at one of his paintings. "His calling card is steel utensils that are the basis of daily life for the rural poor, but I find his work has become a bit repetitive." I breathe an internal sigh of relief that I have instead met underground up-and-coming artists.

Manil was born in Lucknow, but has been in Delhi for eight years. As a child his interests lay not in art but in sport; he even played cricket professionally "but it didn't work out. Now I watch it voraciously and I think it has given me a sense of positivity and discipline, although I believe in moderation not extremes. I will never become an escapist and I won't turn to drugs!" At college he learnt to draw in a very graphic style, which led to commissions of illustrations for fashion and storyboards. "I had thought I wanted to do fashion but realised that it wasn't my cup of tea. I didn't realise I was meant to end up here! There was a very tight government structure at college, so it wasn't productive for contemporary growth – but when I went out to exhibitions I got really excited. I could see myself fitting in and making my own expression. I really enjoy the freedom of being an artist." He only started painting in 2003, when the art market "was looking bright" and enjoys the fact that he doesn't have to think about what end result a client is looking for "so there is the opportunity in my own self to have a dialogue with society." He has been represented by Palette for two years. "The owners have really challenged the art market by putting on bold shows," says Manil. "They are able to do this because they are supported by successful fashion brands. They even help artists with framing and the costs of transport. It's good fun." Living with his wife, he enjoys working alone. "My wife works at the gallery, but we kept it a secret when I first joined."

Painting in acrylic, Manil is gung-ho with his method of application. "I like to keep it spontaneous so there is a thrill from venturing out onto the canvas, making mistakes as I go. It takes me somewhere, and I can add stuff gradually." In Endangered Engender, featuring a multi-limbed headless and heavily pregnant torso, he takes on the stereotype of the goddess and the paradoxes of how different cultures treat the genders. "I use the female goddess form from Indian mythology, but she has broken limbs." Perpetual Calendar Per Square Foot is thick with a conglomerate sprawl of human and animal parts, gaping wounds "all juiced up and splashing like candies – everything is up for consumption." Two particular stumps are pointed out as references to the Twin Towers, and indeed there are some rocket like creations heading towards their mid regions. I ask if this was created with a global audience in mind and he looks aghast. "You can't think of terrorism as only happening in another place [removed from us]. We all know of bombs – it is not a US phenomena at all – we all deal with terrorists and we all witnessed 9/11. No one can isolate themselves." He is referring, in part, to the fatal bomb blasts that occur in Delhi whilst I am there.

Manil is clearly a man who thinks a lot, who worries, who struggles with his conscience. I ask whether he is actively contributing to society with anything beyond his art, and he mentions some workshops he has held at the India Habitat Centre, "but I've stopped for a couple of years to focus on my art." He would like to do more in the future – making interactive works which are shown on a more accessible platform (I can't help feeling that the locked gates which bar the gallery from the great unwashed aren't helping) and he would like to work with an NGO that is involved with the issues that most interest him. "Participation and effort at the individual level are important because you can't talk about issues and do nothing," he admits. "Then it becomes a vain effort."

One striking painting features a headless figure wearing period costume and I can't tell if it is Mughal or Elizabethan, which is apparently the intention. "It is a hybrid theatrical setting, a theatre of the absurd, because life is a stage. I wanted to represent high society vanity." He tries to stay away from obvious folk art inspirations. "Art that is very local in its references becomes too limited." I ask whether the Brothers In Arms title of another painting is a nod in the direction of the famous Dire Straits album and he admits that maybe, subconsciously it is. "I try to keep the titles simple so that I can communicate ideas more easily." In Love No More a sad severed buffalo head represents the "leftover part, but also the most crucial part" of the body. Given that so much of Manil's art is concerned with the consumption of animals, I ask him whether he is vegetarian. "I was fluctuating for a long time because I couldn't find the right answer," he says, "but now I have found my reason for conversion."

Manil struggles to focus on both art and marketing at the same time, so he enjoys meeting up with other artists attending the numerous gallery openings across the scattered Delhi art scene. "A central gathering space for artists is much needed," he mentions. "and I think this will happen with the creation of the Religiare Arts space. But," he sadly informs me, "no beer, I think." As he and his wife are due to leave the gallery at the same time as me they kindly offer me a lift, upon which it saddens me greatly to discover that Manil drives a huge 4 x 4. I don't doubt that his intentions are honourable, but it's all part of the great Indian dichotomy – the middle classes are more aware than ever of their tenuous grasp on a destructive consumerist lifestyle, but they are not yet prepared to take a good long look at their own hard earned luxuries. In fact, this is true across the world. The moneyed classes are by and large afflicted by a peculiar type of blindness that prevents them from associating any of their desires with planetary ruin. We soon become snarled up in the rush hour traffic jams on the commuter belt, so Manil drops me at a busy commuter intersection to fend for myself on the mean streets of Delhi. I hope the much-vaunted new metro system will be all it's cracked up to be, and that Manil and many others will make the most of it.

SADAN PANDE

Sadan Pande is a devout Hindu in an arranged marriage. He is also a highly camp and fantastically funny fashion designer who loves our very own z-list celebrity Jade Goody. His best mate is a twenty two year old gay stylist called Eric. Welcome to modern India.

I first encounter Sadan in the decidedly unglamourous basement environs of the agency who will supply me with models for my fashion shoots. Builders are banging away around us. "We build, we break it, again we build," he comments, deadpan. "Labour is very cheap." An avuncular character, he is wearing an unavoidably bright green top and distinctive red rimmed glasses – a combination that I would like him to wear for our interview, but this will not be possible for tomorrow is a yellow day, and thus it proves to be... We shoot on the rooftop of Sadan's studio in Shahpur Jat, with his friend Ritu as our model. "I will only shoot with her, she'll fit the clothes 300%." Unbelievably she is thirty years old, but doesn't look a day over twenty. Sadan jokes and flirts with her about her 'dusky' skin tone – rare amongst models who are usually light or 'wheatish' in colour – as she stands on a concrete pillar in the approaching dusk and the big ploppy late monsoon raindrops start to fall on her fuschia pink balloon gown. True to cliché the locals crowd around us when we shoot in the street. And gather on their balconies and rooftops. And stop their motorbikes. We finish quickly, just as night falls and a power cut reduces the studio to candlelight. Giving me directions to a coffee shop some blocks away, Sadan rushes off to his temple. Of course I have difficulty finding it, for as usual the auto rickshaw driver doesn't know where it is. Sadan is later still, racing into the café in a flurry and exclaiming "Getting lost is a common occurance here; noone has a clue where anything is." Sitting down he orders a cheese croissant from the decidedly westernized menu, and seeing my expression, explains his choice. "I like this because it has less flavour. Traditional [Indian] food is not necessarily spicy, that's a myth. I'm from Lucknow in Uttar Pradesh, (Uppi for short) and it's an authentic Muslim town with traditional Mughal food; yummy is the word! How can you tolerate the food here?" he asks rhetorically, aghast. For Delhi is a melting pot of Indian cultures, and the food is similarly mixed up. "It's like a concoction, neither here nor there."

At thirty two years old Sadan has already had a long and varied career. By seventeen he had chosen the science stream at school and went on to take an economics degree. "I loved it! But people stress too much about a basic primary education." That's a first degree to you and me. "College becomes a long age-specific process." He loved the theory of economics but dreaded the thought of a lifetime spent in human resources or the Civil Service. So Sadan took the most obvious option and attended the reknowned NIFT, of course. "We were like prisoners of war there, it was like primary school, all our dreams were shattered," he says, happily mixing his metaphors. Then he left and hit the real world, which was even worse. "I was a buying merchandiser in an office; it was so mundane, so boring, a very stereotype 9-9 job." That these hours trip off his tongue says a lot about the new Indian work ethic. Everyone appears to be working all the time. "Every day you do the exact same, with no excitement, nothing new. A lot of people have problems

making friends because they are in competition." Instead he drifted into a successful career as a fashion stylist. "I most liked meeting new sets of people on each shoot, all working towards one goal, getting thrilled by pressure." He loved the travel to exotic places: "I've been to Mughal interior villages, beautiful hills in Rajasthan, amazing beaches. It's great fun to see the real India." It seems somewhat ironic that in order to see the 'real' India one must first work in a totally hectic and stressful but relatively pointless urban job. "I enjoy the lethargy in small towns because here all is running, not even meeting timetables, always late, lagging behind. It's very frustrating because things still don't get done. [Rural Indians] know exactly what they need to do and they work at an awesome pace. They are very peaceful but I don't call them non-aspirational. I enjoy their lifestyle."

Sadan even tried his hand at a bit of celebrity styling. "I did a brief stint in Bollywood. It was a good experience but a very different genre altogether and I am not a celeb celeb designer," he says, "they want clothes that are the prime focus and I don't want to be noticed because of a celebrity." It's clearly a topic that he has a lot to say about. "Celebrities are made by other people, but they think they are born celebs! They all want to be the most gorgeous star in the film but they are just a bunch of insecure people." He then lists off with relish all the procedures they routinely have done: "Nose job, ear, eye, botox – what job they haven't done? That's what needs to be figured out! It even starts with very young new

actresses." A strange – at least to my western taste – put popular option is surgery to create cheek dimples. "Punjabi men are simple with dimples!" he laughs in his singsong lilting voice.

A tall thin trendy young man, sporting a mullet that would not look out of place in arty Hoxton, comes steaming into the café with a bulging bag of fashion magazines. He looks curiously Chinese for an Indian man, but Sadan explains that he is from north eastern India, which is near Mongolia. Flicking through Indian Grazia I come across a model I know from Sweden looking languidly glamourous in a fashion spread, and I marvel at the small world we live in. Indian Idol booms out of the telly hanging in the corner of the café above a couple cooing over their lattes. "I love it! I'm a complete TV buff," claps Sadan. "I love reality shows." I ask him what he thinks about the whole Jade Goody debacle (having just recently announced that she has cancer on India's Bigg Boss show) "She's a victim of the whole thing – she was promised it was off camera but it was false. Reality shows need this, but the shows are always bigger than the people who take part." Shilpa Shetty, however, is now a major star, thanks to her stint on our Big Brother. "Everyone knows who she is. She has evolved as a person, become more intellectual. Now she is cutting albums on yoga and spiritual advice... and her dress is very nice." Would he like Shilpa to wear his clothes? "I would love her to! I love her figure, love her eyes. When that kind [of celeb] wears your stuff you feel good, but I wouldn't

give my clothes to a bimbo in Bollywood. She only has her bimbo status because of shedding her clothes so what does it matter what she wears?!"

Eventually the exciting life of a jobbing stylist lost its allure, despite the considerable salary of 35,000 rupees a day (approximately £450 at the time of writing). "I got stuck in shoots that I didn't want to do – I was constantly amazed that you are hired as a professional, yet you meet people with no knowledge and much much bigger egos who try to force their point of view on you." Inspired by his love of "kaleidoscopic patterns of dancing colours" Sadan decided to launch his own label for the "modern assertive Indian woman who can make her own decision of what to wear. There used to be lots of dos and don'ts but now people are ready to experiment." His plans involve getting into a main fashion event like Lakme Fashion Week in Bombay (no one calls it Mumbai) but it is hard to get into such illustrious occasions. "There is so much scheming! You need many social contacts, good PR, backing. And I am a very bad marketing person. I can sell other things but I can't sell myself!" Eventually he has ambitious plans to set up a design house "with my methodology and philosophy." It would sell Sadan Pande branded accessories and interiors. I wonder if the vegetable print dyes he uses are a conscious concession to our spiraling environmental predicament. "I tell you what, to a certain extent yes, wherever I can I am keen to do something because [climate change] is already affecting us. But I have financial constraints so for now I am

more market driven."

Sadan has no problem mixing Hinduism with his high fashion lifestyle. "When God has planned something then it will come to me." He does puja every morning without fail, attending the temple as early as 6.45am, no matter what else he has to do. And on Thursdays he attends extra prayers in the mid afternoon, hence the postponement of our interview. How on earth does he manage to fit such devotion into his schedule? "I am very good with my time management, and I feel bad if I miss it. I like to spend my morning with a little meditation for the day so I read the newspaper at my own speed with two big cups of chai to get in that peaceful mode." He hasn't met many people in the business who are as devout as he is but he is proud of his beliefs. "I am answerable to all that I do, which makes one a beautiful human being." As we leave the café to take autos home I also discover that he got married a year ago, to a graphic designer approved by the family. "I don't love her," he guilelessly informs me, "but I like her and I don't regret it. I'm a Libran so I like to adapt. How come you guys are so specific in what you want?!" Indeed, too much choice could be a bad thing... Eric takes the opportunity to try and persuade Sadan to join him for a night out on the tiles, "I make him forget he has a wife!" he chortles. "All young boys can go out all night," replies Sadan good-naturedly. "You'll cause my divorce!" I leave the unlikely (or maybe not so) pair to sort out the clashing social realities so typical of modern India.

ADVAITA

Anindo, erstwhile keyboardist and producer of the band Advaita, lives at home with his parents, where he has converted a front room into a heavily soundproofed professional studio – professional that is, apart from the foul stench of drains that I do my best to ignore. I arrive as lunch is being served and the newspaper laid out on the glass coffee table is abruptly whisked away so that we can eat in more style. Anindo is a serious young fellow, a teetotal workaholic. "I literally live in the studio," he says, "waiting for the album to hatch." "This is the beehive," laughs guitarist Abhishek. Most of the band still live at home and take full advantage of familial generosity. "All our parents are really supportive – they sponsor us to stare at the ceiling for two or three years," he says. "You move on and get independent at a younger age in the UK." I think he may overestimate the independence of the great British youth – putting off a 'real job' is clearly a global phenomenon.

Advaida means "everything is one", an apt name for a band determined to mix up a whole host of influences. "We don't like being called fusion though – it's annoying," says Anindo. Fusion music, used for several decades to describe any kind of east/west confluence of styles, has become a dirty word in cool Indian music circles. "We're chasing a sound that we can't quite pinpoint," says guitarist Abhishek. "We love Pink Floyd and The Chemical Brothers, but we also use tabla rhythms." That eastern melodies should bump along against western lyrics and vice versa seems perfectly logical in this global age. "We have more in common with people in cities across the world than with those who live in rural India," he explains. "Urban areas are points of energy from which the stream of influences goes both ways; western culture is very powerful and we react to that. Rock music is not identified with any one place: let's put our colonial past behind us." The spectre of British rule is never far away, for these young men, like everyone I meet in Delhi, speak Hinglish all day everyday. Sometimes this curious hybrid of archaic English and native language is hard to understand,

but for the most part it makes communication much easier than in other countries I have visited – although it takes me awhile to decipher the vague sideways head wobble that in the UK would mean no, but to Indians means 'yes', or in some cases 'yes... maybe'.

Clean cut classical singer Ujwan and tabla player Mohit describe the complex use of preset notes in ragas and the importance of mood in Indian traditional music. "The mood is always very explicit – for example, there is a 'slightly happy in the evening in summer' melody. And it's like a joke for us that so many songs are based on rain!" According to Indian convention rain equates with happiness but in a western-influenced reversal of the norm many bands now use rainy metaphors to intimate sadness too. I ask if it was intentional to form an all male band, and Abhishek somewhat mournfully says that "from a presentation point of view it would be nice to have a girl" but that they were not able to find a decent female singer. Instead they perform on occasion with a female classical dancer, which seems to go down well with an audience that spans young and old.

Advaita are very much part of a niche scene, but having turned down an offer made by the massive Indian music company Saregama (HMV to you and me) "they specified that we couldn't get married during the promotional phase! Business in India is very messed up," the band are keen to do things their own way. Touring on the university circuit they have attracted the interest of legendary British producer John Leckie, with whom they hope to record. Whilst 50,000 musicians live off the Bollywood industry in Mumbai, Delhi is the epicentre of the underground scene, and for cool young middle-class Indians like Advaita the once staple diet of covers is out; a new era of experimental fusion music has begun.

MySpace: advaitamusic

ists that I was able to find in India. Many produce work that just isn't to my taste; twee art to which I can't relate, either aesthetically or mentally. Exasperated, I had trawled through Indian Art News in the hope of finding something inspiring, and that was when I chanced upon Kanak, lurking between the mannered rural scenes and laboured abstract art. Even viewed on a small screen the vibrancy of her paintings; intimate portrayals of private moments awash with unutterable emotion and mute pain, had me captivated. I joined the website in the hopes of being able to contact this mysterious woman and was rewarded with an immediate response. That same afternoon I find myself sitting on a cushion, flipping through Hindi children's magazines.

Kanak grew up in Madhya Pradesh state, a child of liberal parents – her father is involved in education and her mother championed the women's movement. During the 80's her mother worked for an organisation involved in putting together the first graded reading series for Hindi speaking kids, and on finishing her fine art degree in Gujarat Kanak went to work with them on educational material. Playful papercut cats and loosely inked inquisitive hens dance across the pages of slim volumes aimed at primary age children. "I love illustrating for kids," she says delightedly, "but after a while I needed more challenges for my work."

Now twenty eight years old, Kanak has only recently moved to Delhi to make a career in art, unfettered by her past. I wonder what prompted the move and Kanak, sheepishly, but also somewhat gleefully, declares that there is something she must tell me. With a curious glint in her eye she relishes the momentary pause. For Kanak used to be a boy. As a child she was cute and girly. "It is common in Indian familes, when a kid is affectionate, to call them by a female name." Everyone thought she was a girl acting like a boy, but as she grew up things became more uncomfortable. "Nobody pays you any respect when you are a very feminine male and people used to think I was gay which I really hated. I've never enjoyed any of the privelages of being a man because I've never felt like a man." On graduating from college, having always acted and felt like a female, Kanak

I have trouble locating Kanak's flat, tucked away as it is in a gated enclave in the unending stretches of characterless suburbia that radiate out from central Delhi. At the top of a twisting flight of stairs, past the late afternoon family chatterings emanating from each passed floor, I eventually find Kanak smiling prettily in the doorway to her sparse but daintily decorated studio-cum-living space. Around us, huge bold paintings are propped up against the mint green walls, spectacular in their personal intensity.

Maybe I should explain at this point that shortly before I met Kanak I had become increasingly worried about the type of art-

KANAK SHASHI

made the brave decision to take a few years off from her burgeoning career so that she might make a name for herself as a woman.

Her former name meant revolution. What made her choose the name Kanak? "I wanted a name that sounded like the goddess Kaly-ani," she says "something balanced that can be read from both sides." Thus she renamed herself with the palindrome Kanak. With money earned from the sales of her artwork Kanak went home to Madhya Pradesh and set about her transformation. "I had some minor surgery in India and the windows in the operating theatre were open so all the flies came inside; it was sick," she says candidly. Her final operation was performed in Bangkok.

Unsurprisingly, Kanak is intrigued by the place of women in family and society, and of what it means to belong. She is attracted to inspiring female characters from every walk of life, from the street whores of the shanty towns to familiar celebrities. "I look for strong women to portray; this one shows a famous singer whose voice I love," she says, showing me a huge painting of three women gathered around a microphone. "She is extremely tiny, but she has a hold over all of India." The figures show this singer at different ages, ever powerful. "She has always been single, she never married and didn't have kids. I can relate to this strength." I wonder if Kanak is fond of children. "They're nice if they belong to someone else," she giggles, "but I have a girl cat now and I wouldn't mind kittens in the house!" Cats feature widely in Kanak's paintings, for they represent "comfort, family and home." As if on cue her rangy cat comes roaming into the room, so we both coo awhile over the delicate nervy creature.

On another canvas unfurled upon the floor a fat lady hangs out in the park whilst a thin "model shadow" version of herself stretches accusingly across the ground. "But she is happy, smiling, cheerful! Why should she lose weight?!" cries Kanak. Another muse is a famously beautiful actress. "She was in her late thirties when she did this movie in which everyone said she looked ugly, but she was so great in it that she overpowered every other actor." Kanak was frequently sent sketching in the slums near her college. "You need a high tolerance to go in there. I would sit and gossip with this one woman who was like a king."

In a cosy painting titled Family Picture Kanak re-imagines what the concept of family means. Inspired by the real lifestyle of a lesbian couple that are family friends, it conjures up one of those wonderfully blissful moments of the type that many people, including those in more conservative familial arrangements, find it hard to attain. "They helped me out a lot," she says, "and I really liked the atmosphere in their house – they've created a new kind of family." As the couple sit relaxing with a book and their cat in what look like pyjamas, a severe traditional pairing gazes down dispiritedly from a photograph on the wall above. For the striking paintings Opting To Perform A Boy and Opting To Perform A Girl Kanak took inspiration from American posters from the 1950's which show how one should behave around the house. It is telling that both paintings clearly feature a girl, with the 'boy', clad in a puffy pink frock, looking somewhat flummoxed by the football that has been placed on his lap.

It was only after Kanak became the girl she always knew she was that she finally felt happy to paint herself, and it is these most recent paintings that I found on Indian Art News. Made from pho-

a motorbike drew alongside – bear in mind that this is at high speed on the freeway – and, taking his hand off the handlebar, grabbed lewdly at my thigh. What he hoped to achieve short of a James Bond style leap into my rickshaw wherein he would harass me still further, I have no idea, but it left me feeling defiled. Luckily my trusty rickshaw driver put his foot to the pedal and managed to muster up enough speed to put some distance between us, but it left me pondering the subject of objectification.

We now turn towards the only painting that was done during Kanak's period of transition, a time when she found it very hard to focus on her work. In this painting, which has no name, a faceless man hugs a woman, her eyes wide with worry, her arms entwined with his. "The man is a friend of mine that I was having a relationship with at the time. We were living together as friends... but with sexual relations," she explains. "The sex was never a very conscious move, but somehow it would happen and then we wouldn't talk about it or accept it during the day... I wanted an affirmation that I was desirable but I just felt so much emptiness." Like many of her paintings this one is full of triangular shapes "because they are containing and have no particular direction, so they echo my feelings." This man could not accept who Kanak was. "He didn't want to think of himself as a homosexual and he was too conservative to accept the situation, so he became more and more depressed." The pain this confused man caused Kanak is palpable. "I'm not looking for a boyfriend right now even though I gets lots of proposals. I am always worried about what will happen when I tell the truth because I can't take rejection anymore," she sighs wistfully. Despite or maybe because of her situation, Kanak is incredibly good at articulating the universal doubt, fear and pain to which we can all relate.

Although Kanak is relatively new to the arts scene in Delhi she has already had some promising meetings with scouts from top galleries who have expressed an interest in her. "The biggest gallery has taken four of my paintings on consignment to show to potential buyers, but they've had them for a year now and I don't know when I'll get them back," she says.

tographs taken by friends, they are questioning of the male gaze, of what exactly it is that men find so intriguing about a female body. "Why are men so interested in a woman's body, her feet, her cleavage? What exactly is it that is so special?" she asks. "Why are men so violently curious that they must tease women?" The teasing Kanak speaks of is not the mild sort associated with playful flirting, but intimidating predatory teasing of the kind that is still rife in India. "There is a big culture of harassment here; men follow you in a car, offer you something." Having experienced it myself on my short trip up to see Kanak, I am pleased finally to have a name to put to the practice. In India 'Eve teasing' is sexual harassment of the most insidious form, encompassing anything from sexually suggestive remarks to outright groping. As I sat in my auto rickshaw a man on

Many of her art school contemporaries were lucky enough to graduate just as the modern art boom gained momentum two years ago, and Kanak expresses concern that she has missed this crucial opportunity. Yet she is eager to make it on her own terms, and balks at the suggestion, made by both her liberal parents and her friends, that she should "do a Frida Kahlo" and describe the minutae of her many operations on canvas. "I don't want to be trapped inbetween," she affirms. "I want to be a normal woman." And I am sure that make it she will, as a 'normal' woman who is capable of expressing the most subtle of female emotions with amazing skill.

SAMANT CHAUHAN

Samant Chauhan is twenty nine years old, a workaholic, dedicated to making it on his own terms in the complex world of Indian contemporary fashion. Considered one of India's most avante-garde young designers he is a media darling and a busy man with several catwalk shows imminent, and his mobile is glued to his ear as I take a photo in the narrow lane outside his humble studio in the Shahpur Jat textiles district so popular with fashion designers. Stepping inside his tiny office I am hit with the intense heat of so many bodies beavering away in such a small room and in order to stay cool we retire to the large clothing cupboard which holds his acclaimed Kama Sutra collection; with the aircon turned on full throttle it is icy cool, like stepping inside a giant walk-in fridge. Two of his friends sit interestedly on the window sill as I ask him a few questions.

Samant hails from the small town of Bhagalpuri in Bihar, where his father works on the railways. "He always encouraged me to follow my dreams because he knows that there is a limited source of income in what he does, but with fashion there is the possibility that I can earn a lot of money," he explains. Following the obligatory completion of a 'serious' degree in physics he won a place at NIFT where he specialised in knitwear. "My graduate collection was selected for Singapore Fashion Week, where I won a prize which allowed me to start up my own label," he says. "Once I graduated I started to work for an export fashion house, and my consultancy continues to supplement my the income from my own label."

Despite being a critically-garlanded contemporary designer, his collections have yet to make any significant profits because he refuses to kowtow to the fashion designer's staple, an overwhelming use of embroidered embellishments. "It's a very difficult market because most customers just don't appreciate good cut and finish, although there is a growing market of modern open-minded young people who want my designs."

Samant, determined to save the livelihoods of the raw silk handloom weavers in his hometown of Bhagalpuri, works from the ground up, using only the finest natural handspun silk hand sourced from local farms. "The weavers used to make fabrics for home furnishings, but this is no longer commercially realistic," he says. "I want to help them produce fabrics that will reach a global audience." So raw silk forms the heart of all Samant's designs, which dare to challenge traditional Indian tastes with a predominantly cream and neutral colour palette of delicate rough-edged knits layered over unusual rippled dresses. Undaunted by the difficult menswear market he also offers a large menswear collection, dominated by large scale abstract prints meshed with natural woven silk in a multitude of variations. His unique sensibilities and environmentally aware approach helped to win him a discounted stand at the Esthetica stands at London Fashion Week earlier this year, but funding is scarce and it is a trip that is expensive to make as often as he would like.

Unlike many other designers Samant does not have a family business to fall back on and "money to waste," hence his workaholic nature. "It's not okay," he replies when I ask if he enjoys working so hard, "but I have no other option. Maybe in another year I'll be able to relax a little bit." And does he like living in Delhi, I wonder? "Not exactly... I have no family here,

but I go home once a year for a festival in November." His friends joke that he goes home "for Christmas" in a nod to my British sensibilities. Like many people of his generation Samant has become displaced in his pursuit of a satisfying career that would not have been possible for his father's generation, but at what cost? He occasionally gets out to the movies, and in an unexpected twist he is now designing the entire wardrobe and sets for an art film about the life of the famous smuggler Veerappan, a notorious elephant poacher and looter of sandalwood who eluded the police across several states for twenty years. In typical Indian style the film features a cast of six hundred, of which a mere sixty eight are main characters. "I've had to think about everything from their pistols to the kind of food they eat. It's really exciting to see how a film director considers so much detail – reading the script is like watching a movie." He notes that thinking in such a different way has affected the way

he visualises his own collections. "Now when I design for the catwalk I feel as though I am writing a script."

Thanks to some funding from the Fashion Design Council of India, Samant is due to hit the famous catwalks, or "ramps" of Paris shortly after my visit. "Most people can't believe that I will be showing in the Louvre since they know how expensive it is!" he exclaims, thrilled at his good luck. But the fact is, Samant is one of very few contemporary Indian designers who are determined to push against the acceptable parameters of high fashion, and the powers-that-be clearly recognise that they have a formidable talent on their hands, whether or not he is yet making a dent in the commercial side of the domestic market. It is indeed a wise move to send him abroad, where his designs are ironically much more likely to gain not only recognition but those crucial sales that are so hard to come by in India.

EMPEROR MINGE

MySpace: mingeemperor

The improbably named Emperor Minge are practicing, crammed into a tiny tiny rehearsal room at the Performing Arts School in downtown Delhi. I had planned to see them live, but the gig was cancelled in a government crack down on all public gatherings following the terrorist attacks that rocked the city. My ears are nearly blasted off by the proximity of singer Parvati, who is ear-shatteringly close. A large girl, she is dressed in a strapless black formal dress topped with an unbecoming orange vest. "I'm not taking it off if we're shooting outside," she informs me in no uncertain terms. "You ain't never going down on my (choot ch ch choo ch ch choot) ever again (choot just a fucking choot)," she sings. Written by Brit beatnik poet Jamie Kelsey and sent via Skype to Stefan K – the forty-odd years old English expat mastermind behind Emperor Minge – the lyrics refer to the Hindi slang for a vagina. "We like pushing boundaries," says Stefan. "It's supposed to be about Bush but... it's fun. People think we are talking about locomotives."

On MySpace Stefan cites his inspirations as "love, the speaking clock, pigeons in the aircon shaft, sex, Situationism, Hitchcock, the birds and the bees, mortality and the Village People... probably." It is indeed hard to pin down the Emperor Minge sound, something which Stefan delights in, along with their thoroughly ridiculous name. "Stefan couldn't pronounce our first vocalist's name," explains drummer Nikhil, "so he called her Minger, not that any of us knew what it meant back then. We decided to name the band after Charles Mingus, but then Mingus Dynasty turned into Emperor Minge in honour of her. It was only a working title but by then it was too late..." "And anyway, we're a cheeky band so it fits," adds Stefan.

Stefan, an accomplished musician, has been pursuing fame and fortune for many years: along with Jamie he was a key member of the now defunct London art band The Peoples' Friend, but being a man with frisky feet he then spent five years working in the theatre in Barcelona before moving to India. "It turned out a bit different to how I imagined," he says, in his po-faced manner. "I've barely touched a sitar and I've stopped watching Bollywood films." Instead he has turned his attentions to forming the kind of band that Delhi never knew it was waiting for.

With practice over for the moment, we head out onto the mean side streets of Delhi to take a photo of Emperor Minge, but it's hard work to catch the entire band from a good angle. Stefan, more practiced in such matters, is happy to take direction, but I am unaccustomed to the lack of enthusiasm shown by Parvati, clearly a diva in the making – she moans about feeling ill and looks sullen throughout. It is all I can do to persuade her to come along for the interview. Once settled in a coffee shop some blocks away she begins to defrost, but now it is Stefan's turn to throw a strop. He's unhappy about the lemon soda he has ordered, and he won't let up even though the poor waiter has clearly been given strict instructions not to deviate from brand policy.

Nikhil met Stefan at a gig not long after he arrived in India. "We discovered that we share the same vision; which is to stand out as a truly original musical act, with great visual stage presentation," clarifies Nikhil, who is a virtuoso session musician more used to playing in the light jazz and fusion outfits that are so popular in Delhi. Together they have made it their raison d'etre to avoid creating anything that they've heard before. Parvati has a vast wealth of experience singing in both classical and western bands, and she was formerly a member of Artists Unlimited; a well known vocal collective that sings covers of western songs. It was here that she met her best friend Rohit, who is the guitarist with Emperor Minge. This is the first time she has had total freedom to sing how she likes. "I sing in a different manner for every performance," she says, "Stef usually gives me a guide but I don't follow it. I go off on my own tangent. He always lets me know what he thinks and sometimes I hate him but then I wake the up the next morning thinking 'he's so sweet'. I respect what he says because he has greater technical knowledge."

This doesn't stop her plaguing him with suggestions, as I saw in the rehearsal I sat in upon. "I want the others to feel ownership of the band," explains Stefan. "It starts with me but it doesn't end with me." Jamie is currently threatening to come over from England and take on the role of lead vocals, but "he might get featured vocals if he's lucky." I can't see Parvati lightly renouncing her spot.

We talk about what is expected of virtuouso performers in India, where the classical tradition dictates that one must stick to a particular melody. As a result improvisation has become highly prized, with long solos at the forefront. "It's all about powerchords," says Nikhil. "But we don't need to fall back on pyrotechnical virtuosity." Instead they have managed to annoy several venue owners by turning up unannounced with an Egyptian bellydancer in tow. "It's nice to have the attention taken away from me," says Parvati, who is no sex bomb. "Then I can lose myself in the music." And the crowd loves it.

By Stefan's own admission he has made some perverse decisions in his life. Is India a good place to be if you want to be a rock star? "Music is definitely what's keeping me here – within a short space of time we've had lots of attention," he replies. "I get the sense that we are paving the way for others to do something interesting, although some bands don't seem to like us much. I think they feel threatened [by us] because they'll be obsolete if we become successful." He'd love to reach an international level of recognition with the band, but I wonder if being in India is not counterintuitive to this idealogy. "It's not without its challenges but in general I like being here. It's a huge city and there's not too much competition, so for some strange reason I thought I could make it big here..." I am highly doubtful that Stefan has the necessary savvy to make it, but I wish them all the best, for Emperor Minge are without question one of the most unique and exciting bands in India right now. And I think I've just spotted a sitar on one of their new songs.

On my last day, with high hopes of meeting a community fostering the perfect combination of ecology and arts, I decide to pay a visit to the Global Arts Village in the outskirts of Delhi... But this isn't quite what greets me at the end of one very long auto rickshaw ride, which includes being told that I am "precious and sexy" when we stop to ask for directions. I am somewhat flummoxed to find that, having bounced down an eerily quiet driveway, I appear to be at the gates of a large private mansion. Except the smiling guard at the doorway knows my name. On entering the manicured grounds I am taken down a curving pathway towards a large tented celebration area in the middle of which is a small group of people picking at the remains of their lunch. Unsure of what to do with myself I sit down in the circle and make my introductions. A bustling community it ain't.

For this 'Arts Village' is actually one rich man's vision. It may not be what I expected, but an eye-opener it surely is; yet another part of the perplexing duality of modern India. The owner Ashwin is long-haired, relaxed in casual western clothes, with a soothing but slightly pained expression – one that is riven with guilt. A man whose small personal fortune, removed from his family's garment business, is being spent in the pursuit of something more meaningful than the production of cheap clothes. It's a predicament I recognise well – the overwhelming urge to do something of consequence in this big ol' confusing world of ours. To this end he has created a curious haven, a place of retreat for artists and seekers, built on ecological ideas dictated by the ancient Indian art of Vaastu, which relates design principles to earth energies. Smiling ladies with cleaning buckets scurry past me as I am shown around the beautiful empty apartments. The main building, built a decade ago, is a blue tiled modern masterpiece, an airy atrium to dreams. But we walk past it down a grassed path towards where Ashwin is building his new environmentally sound dream house. A wiry dark man is squat, engrossed in picking out tiny grass seedlings one by one. I ask why and am told that they are the wrong type of grass; indeed they are marginally thicker-leaved than the surrounding spindly grasses. I think: labour is very cheap here. Of course this is fact, but the reality of it is like a smack in the face. This community is not like others I have visited closer to home, where everyone pitches in with domestic duties; it's a community of master and servants, and visitors.

Of which twenty six year old Rachel Immanuel is one. Sitting at a long low lovingly-made wooden table with water tinkling outside the open window, we scroll through images on her laptop. Trained in both contemporary art practice and graphic design, "I navigated courses for five years," she lives in her hometown of Bangalore, where she was recommended to apply for a sponsorship at the village by her college director. "This place lets you be," she explains, "I need a lot of space and this is great for that, plus it has workshops that I can use." A damning indictment to India's adoption of western values, Rachel's Buy't project includes a magazine and screen print series that take a look at the role of women in modern India, with specific regard to what she calls the "snake of consumerism." The work showcases her technique, which involves manipulating – "It's collaging!" I get a withering look – photographic imagery in Photoshop. It's clear that Rachel does not suffer fools gladly. "We now worship the goddesses of education and money. They give us status, but not without cost. There is a paradox at work." Rachel is not at all sure that this modern woman thing is all it's cracked up to be. "You are either a good wife or a vamp, and there is nothing in between," she says. "Women are tortured – to be a so-called liberated women in India is really hard. The cosmetics companies have sold us a dream, but there are still such strong social pressures here that the border between a loose and a modern women has not been properly delineated." And where has it? One major legacy of the emancipation of women has been mindless and soul-destroying promiscuity, and that holds true across the world. However, other nations do not also have to

Rachel IMMANUEL

contend with the "extremely heavy male gaze," of the type that I experience many times during my stay and indeed on my way to the village. Rachel is shocked to discover that I travel around Delhi on my own, a single woman. "I don't like oppression in any form," she explains, "but it is really dangerous to travel alone here."

To avoid undue 'Eve-teasing' Rachel has been making research trips into town with the young female photographer who is the only other guest at the village. Her new artworks are once more based on the collision of cultures. "The contrast of old and new in Delhi is obvious everywhere," she asserts. Muslim motifs bounce against Hindu imagery, the Coca-Cola byline 'life ho to aisi' (meaning 'that's what life should be like!') is embedded on city walls above beggars, young men lounge idly in prisoner-stripe T-shirts in front of gigantic generic office blocks. Rachel is obsessed by change, how we adapt to it. In another striking black and white image a bicycle seat is held aloft as if on a pedestal, symbolic of its greatness. "I am interested in the duality of bicycles: they are eco friendly... but here they also represent lower standards because they are a symbol of the lower class. And it shouldn't be like that when the truth is the opposite to reality!" More than once otherwise sensible Indians look at me as if I am barking mad when I tell them that I no longer have a car, that a bike suits me just fine in London.

Several bombs have gone off in Delhi in the past few days, most likely the doing of religious fanatics. "The extreme religious reality that we live in just gets worse and worse," she says "and it's just so unnecessary to be divided by religion or class." I wonder whether she herself is religious, and get a scathing look, as if to say don't I realise she has a Christian name? Obviously Rachel is a very biblical name and all, but I have never ascribed any great meaning to the etymology of names. Rachel, despite her heritage, prefers to mix up her beliefs – so that the Virgin Mary happily rubs shoulders with multi-limbed Hindu deities in her artwork.

"I don't like to be bogged down by any restrictive systems," says Rachel. She is especially unhappy with any borders to do with class. "There used to be a feudal system here, so now we just assume that everyone has a certain place due to an age old history of oppression." This very delineation of society is especially obvious in the Global Arts Village, but everywhere I go I encounter the casual manner with which servile labour is accepted. Yet Rachel is the first person that I have met who is happy to talk about this last taboo, so present and yet so uncommented upon by all the middle class Indians that I meet. "I feel extremely uncomfortable about it [here] because I am not used to it – at home I wash my own dishes and clean my room." Brought up by a liberal father, a psychiatrist and counsellor, her family was the exception and not the norm. When her mother's family sent them a driver her father felt so guilty that he sent the driver's kids to school. This kind of philanthropic attitude has clearly rubbed off on Rachel, who will return to Bangalore to work with a local company on ways

to improve local education and welfare in the area. "It's about helping those around you. If you see the potential in someone then you should push it," she says sensibly "not just keep them there." This reminds me of my experience earlier in the week, when I am invited back to a young man's house (no, not like that!) and have to hide my shock at the way he speaks to the family's help. In an attempt to glean more information about this encounter I ask him whether the servants are his friends, since he has grown up alongside some of the younger ones. "Yes, of course," he replies. "They know exactly how to iron my shirt the way I like it." I'm sorry, but that's not friendship! "One of them is very ambitious," he says as I lean in, excited to hear about some new opportunity for this young man. "He really wants to be a good cook." The idea that someone from the lower classes might become educated is unheard of for most otherwise liberal people. The poor, for the most part, stay poor. New India is another world, a world for the moneyed consuming elite.

"We all speak about equality and we all have utopian ideas, but it is not that easy to change the reality because it means breaking such huge patterns, which is just not the done thing to do. But a slight shift makes all the difference," says Rachel. "Life is stifled by divisions, and like plants we will die because of restrictions." Rachel is determined to stay true to her ideals. "I can't deal with things when they don't mean anything to me – I need to really feel something. I have this idea of utopia in my head but.... mentally Indians have not yet caught up with the boom. It's all happening too fast." Rachel – a bolshy young woman who speaks directly from the heart. She's a tough one to interview, but for her courage and honesty I have the utmost respect.

Fashion

A Child Of The Jago 020 7377 8694
Agent Provocateur 020 7439 0229 www.agentprovocateur.com
Albam www.albamclothing.com
Alessandro Dell'Acqua at Feathers 020 7243 8800
Alexander McQueen 020 7355 0080 www.alexandermcqueen.com
Aminaka Wilmont 020 7514 9354 www.aminawilmont.com
Anna Vince at Browns Focus 020 7514 0063 www.annavince.com
Ann-Sofie Back at B Store 020 7734 6846 www.bstorelondon.com
Ashish 020 8969 6841 www.ashish.co.uk
Atticus www.ebtm.com
B Store www.bstorelondon.com
Bang Bang 020 7631 4191
Baptise from Retro Man 020 7792 1715
Baracuta www.baracuta-g9.com
Barbour www.barbour.com
Ben Sherman 02838 324 121
Bernard Wilhelm at B Store 020 7734 6846
Beyond Retro 020 7613 3636 www.beyondretro.com
Bjork McElligott www.bjorkandmcelligott.com
Bobbin Bicycles 020 7837 3370 www.bobbinbicycles.co.uk
Bora Aksu for People Tree 020 7739 9659 www.peopletree.co.uk
Bryce D'Anice Aime 020 7313 9935 www.bryce-danice-aime.com
Buddhist Punk www.buddhistpunk.co.uk
Cacharel at Liberty 020 7734 1234 www.cacharel.fr
Carhartt 020 7836 1551 www.carhartt-streetwear.com
Carin Wester 0049 30 4201 9200 www.carinwester.com
Christopher Kane at Browns 020 7514 0000 www.brownsfashion.com
Comme des Garçons for H&M www.hm.com
Cooperative Designs www.cooperative-designs.com
Cornelia +46 545 005 50 www.scandinavianpressroom.com
Cyclodelic www.cyclodelic.com
DKNY 020 7499 6238 www.dkny.com
Eley Kishimoto at Liberty 020 7734 1234 www.eleykishimoto.com
Emilio de la Morena www.emiliodelamorena.com

Emma Cook 020 7514 0063 www.brownsfashion.com
Erotokritos 0845 094 4012
Falke at My Tights 0845 004 8400 www.mytights.com
Fifi Bijoux 0141 339 8943 www.fifibijoux.com
Fogal 020 7235 3115
Franklin and Marshall 020 7739 4355 www.franklinandmarshall.com
Fred Butler www.fredbutlerstyle.com
Freddy 020 7836 5291
Galjon 07949 533 601
Giles at Selfridges 0800 123 400 www.selfridges.com
Gossypium www.gossypium.co.uk
H&M www.hm.com
Hans Madsen 020 7493 9600
Hardy Amies www.hardyamies.com
howies 01239 614122 www.howies.co.uk
Issey Miyake Pleats Please 020 7495 2306 www.pleatsplease.com
Just Cavalli at Harrods 020 7730 1234
JW Anderson www.j-w-anderson.com
Katharine Hamnett www.katharinehamnett.com
Kenzo www.kenzo.com
Kenzo Defile by Antonio Marras 0207 225 1960 www.kenzo.com
Kenzo Jeans 0207 225 1960 www.kenzo.com
Krystof Strozyna www.krystofstrozyna.com
KTZ 020 8960 3736 www.kokontozai.co.uk
Lacoste www.lacoste.com
Laitinen at Agentur V +49 30 42019200 www.agenturv.de
Leju 020 8245 7570 www.lejudesigns.com
Les Prairies De Paris at Aime 0207 221 7070
Levis 01604 599 735 www.levi.co.uk
Little Shilpa 07766 092049 www.littleshilpa.com
Lou Dalton 020 7493 9600
Louis Vuitton 020 7399 4050 www.louisvuitton.com
Louise Gray www.louisegrayfashion.com
Lowlife 01323 746 990 www.lowlife.com